About th

Solitaire has been trying to make tl

years. As co-founder of the change agency Futerra, she advises governments, charities and big brands like Danone and L'Oréal on ways to solve social and environmental problems. With Futerra offices now in London, Stockholm, New York and Mexico City, she admits that making the world a better place was a damn good business plan. You can watch her TEDx talks online and read her in the *Guardian*, *Huffington Post* and more often as @GreenSolitaire on Twitter. She was even profiled once in *Harper's Bazaar*, but they didn't let her keep the clothes.

Solitaire would like you to know that yes, she thinks it's a pretty name too. And no, she wasn't named after the Bond girl.

THE HAPPY HERO

THE HAPPY HERO

SOLITAIRE TOWNSEND

Unbound

This edition first published in 2017

Unbound

6th Floor Mutual House, 70 Conduit Street, London W1S 2GF

www.unbound.com

ISBN (eBook): 978-1911586388

ISBN (Paperback): 978-1911586395

Design by Futerra

To Grace, Wynter and Alanna,

for making me want to be a hero.

Dear Reader,

The book you are holding came about in a rather different way to most others. It was funded directly by readers through a new website: Unbound.

Unbound is the creation of three writers. We started the company because we believed there had to be a better deal for both writers and readers. On the Unbound website, authors share the ideas for the books they want to write directly with readers. If enough of you support the book by pledging for it in advance, we produce a beautifully bound special subscribers' edition and distribute a regular edition and e-book wherever books are sold, in shops and online.

This new way of publishing is actually a very old idea (Samuel Johnson funded his dictionary this way). We're just using the internet to build each writer a network of patrons. Here, at the back of this book, you'll find the names of all the people who made it happen.

Publishing in this way means readers are no longer just passive consumers of the books they buy, and authors are free to write the books they really want. They get a much fairer return too – half the profits their books generate, rather than a tiny percentage of the cover price.

If you're not yet a subscriber, we hope that you'll want to join our publishing revolution and have your name listed in one of our books in the future. To get you started, here is a £5 discount on your first pledge. Just visit unbound.com, make your pledge and type IAMAHERO in the promo code box when you check out.

Thank you for your support,

Dan, Justin and John
Founders, Unbound

Super Patrons

Ewelina Abramczuk
Wren Aigaki-Lander
Henrik Åkerman
Patrik Artell
Stina Arvidsson
Lennart Bjurström
Patricia Blalock
Cicely Blalock
Penny Borella
Helen Borland
Mary Ann Brennan
Karen Brennan
Tom Bristow
Sofia Bustamante
Xander Cansell
Yue Cao
Anders Carlborg
Guyang Chen-Ware
Joanna Cholewa
Lech Cholewa
Michal Cholewa
Shruti Choudhary
Ian Christie
Liz Cohen
Myriam Cohen-welgryn
Zoë Coles
Barbara Crowther
Hazel Culley
Harriet Cunningham
Elzbieta Cytawa
Mateusz Cytawa
Peter Davies

Scott Drummond
Peter Enmark
Andy Fisher
Fredrika Fredmark
Gil Friend
Futerra Sustainability Communications Ltd
Alison Garner
Benjamin Gill
Ed Gillespie
Kirsty Gogan
Ruthie Gonzales
Anders Granath
David Grayson
Grzegorz Gurynowicz
Linnea Hellström
Colette Henry
Henry Hicks
Madeleine & Gabrielle Hubert
Kathy Hunter
Laura Hunter
Leslie Isaac
Emilie Ist
Taura Jonaityte
Hannah Jones
Barbara Kaczor
Fredrik Kämpenberg
Wioleta Kazimierczak
Jon Khoo
Dan Kieran
Patrick Kincaid
Heather Knight
Stefan Knutsson
Stefan Kyriazis
Elizabeth LeMay
Niklas Lexén
Anna-Kajsa Lidell

Anton Lilja
Nathalie Lindblom
Clare Lissaman
Magnus Ljungberg
Krista Lowe
Kjell Lundgren
Alistair Macdonald
Amelia Marriette
Anna Matczak
Helen McTaggart
Bartlomiej Misiorek
John Mitchinson
Carl Montelius
Luisa Montes
Dave Newport
Jocelyn Nguyen
Victoria Olausson
Alexandra Palt
Christopher Pinnington
Justin Pollard
Jonathon Porritt
Liz Proctor
Bryony Randall
Ben Robinson
Leticia Rojas
Edith Salminen
Elisabeth Samuelsson
Pawel Sanocki
Alexandra Santiago
Sam Saxby
Mark Schrooten
Lucy Shea
Djani Skrgo
Agne Spangeleviciute
Helen Spoor
Jörgen Staf

Alice Steenland
Kate Stevenson
Andrew Stewart
Meg Sussman
Lukasz Szczyrba
Dariusz Szustak
Hilary Tam
Ariane Thomas
Agnieszka Tomkow
Pia Töre-Wallin
Kaj Török
Patrick Townsend
Deborah Townsend
Sian Townsend
Patrick Townsend
Chris Tuppen
Anne Turner
Diana Velene
Johannes Viebke
Andy Wales
Anders Wallerman
Tomasz Weglewski
Hannah & Simon Whitaker
Charlotte Wightwick
freya Williams
Emma Wood
Jim Woods
Jacek Zbutowicz
Povilas Zigmantas

My Heroes

These people are my Happy Heroes. Thank you for making this book happen.

Yue Cao
Hazel Culley
Kirsty Gogan
Patrick Kincaid
Clare Lissaman
Krista Lowe
Helen McTaggart
Liz Proctor
Helen Spoor
Meg Sussman
Anne Turner

Contents

Introduction: My Promise

Keep your face to the sunshine and you cannot see the shadows.

—Helen Keller

A girl smiles and waves jubilantly at the photographers. She's 13 years old, with fine, mousy hair tousled by the wind. With one hand she's clinging onto the brick monument she's just clambered up, her white pixie boots a little scuffed from the climb. In her other hand she carefully clasps a bag of cheese and onion crisps.

And she's just saved the world.

In the springtime of 1987, the local newspaper, the *Bedfordshire Times*, splashed a photo of that grinning teenager across its centre pages. Its big story was usually about a cat rescued by firemen or the ribbon-cutting ceremony at a shopping centre. But that week, the sleepy English town of Bedford had been the focus of national curiosity. Because after years of political arguments, scientific controversies and local protests, a large company, ominously called Nirex, had announced they were cancelling their plan to build a nuclear-waste 'deep storage facility' in the town.

The local families who had fought so hard against the nuclear-waste dump were taken by surprise. In a flurry of excitement, they gathered at the small brick monument they'd built on the site where Nirex had been planning to store tonnes of radioactive material. Then, as the photographers watched, the families began to accept their success and cry, hug and celebrate. The young girl in the photograph had been swept up in the emotion and scrambled up the bricks. No one really minded the scuff marks or spilled crisps, because most of the people there also felt like climbing, shouting and punching the air. Small folk aren't supposed to beat big corporations, and everyone was a little dazed.

That teenage girl was me. Thankfully, my mother kept the news clipping and had it framed for me. Today it hangs above my desk, and whenever I look up at it, I can vividly remember the moment. I was still a normal teenager, at least on the outside. But that photo captures the instant when my life changed, because that was the first time I truly experienced how good it feels to make a difference. Up on those bricks, with my dad's steadying hand on my ankle, I felt like a superhero who had saved the world.

It was an incredible thrill. And I've learned since, that it was also much more. My feelings at that moment had a strange and extraordinary effect on me. My brain chemistry, my self-esteem and even my future destiny were transformed by that experience. Today, psychologists and neuroscientists are exploring exactly how this phenomenon works – how changing the world can change the person doing it. Of course, I didn't know any of this at the time. It's taken me decades of research and experience to fully understand the power of what I now call 'happy heroism'. And I've written this book to share with you my secret for how *doing* good can be good for *you*. I've also included a lot of advice for really making it happen, no matter where you're starting from. Because I remember how unlike a hero I felt when I began my own adventure.

Two years before the smiling photo in the paper, I'd been hiding in a corner of the school bus, pressed up against the window and trying to avoid the gaze of bullies. One girl was loudly announcing to the whole bus that we were 'going to be nuked', and proceeded to invent horrible deformities for those students sitting nearest to her to suffer. I managed to avoid her gaze, but I did pick up the neon flyer she dropped as she got off the bus. It was from the Bedfordshire Against Nuclear Dumping community group, and it seemed to confirm her dire portents – or at least the part about a planned waste dump. Somehow I couldn't stop thinking about it all that day. The injustice of the situation stirred something in me. So that night I pestered and cajoled my parents into taking me to a meeting. They were pleased I was showing an interest in something other than hiding in my bedroom, although they were a little bemused that my new-found enthusiasm was for a campaign meeting rather than a trip to a sports club or friend's house.

During the meeting my parents themselves became worried to learn about the lack of safeguards and the secret testing that had already started at the dumping site. I was in shock. I couldn't believe that 'big and important adults' were allowing something like this to happen. My resolve hardened and I decided to stick with the other locals in challenging the company. For two years I helped out by making banners and tea. With my now equally dedicated parents at my side and my little sisters playing in the corners of draughty parish halls, we planned our push back. I even did my homework, digging around in the library trying to work out what nuclear waste actually was, and why someone wanted to bury it near my school.

My parents had initially worried that being involved in such a frightening campaign wouldn't be good for an impressionable young teenager. But those two years proved more important to me than anything I had experienced before. It was also the hardest work I'd ever done, and it seemed like it would never end: knocking on neighbours' doors to explain what was happening; long meetings; hours spent each weekend at the protest site, holding banners and waving to passing cars, who beeped their horns in support. My initial enthusiasm slowly became a dogged determination to simply keep going.

And then, suddenly and unexpectedly, we won. The company issued a terse press release saying that they were cancelling plans to bury nuclear waste in our town, or indeed anywhere. The damaging media coverage and public criticism had just been too much. Maintaining that pressure on Nirex had been hard work for everyone involved in the campaign. I'd sacrificed my weekends and evenings to stuff envelopes and make phone calls to politicians. I'd also learned to negotiate with adults, and found that even overwhelmed and exhausted grown-ups can be motivated by a wide-eyed kid innocently asking: 'But we're still going to win, right?'

On reflection, my parents were right: it was a risky lesson for an impressionable teenage girl. By my 14th birthday, I was a seasoned optimist. I firmly believed that if something in the world needs to change, then by staying cheerful and working hard you can change it. Of course, my home town's win against the nuclear-dumping company wasn't global news. Saving one community didn't save the whole world. And although I had been a plucky little campaigner, the Bedfordshire Against Nuclear Dumping campaign had real leaders and officials. But as I sat atop that monument, with a pounding heart and my packet of crisps, I felt like a true hero.

That first experience of changing things for the better unquestionably changed me. As the years passed, I came to realise that trying to make a difference had improved my own life in incalculable ways. The 13-year-old in the newspaper photo looks healthy, independent and optimistic. She's a girl who goes to libraries and understands the rewards of hard work, a happy kid who anyone might guess had the chance of a good life ahead of her. But that wasn't how I'd started out. In the celebration photo, you can see almost no trace of the 11-year-old on the school bus who was terrified of other children and of 'being nuked'. That lost little girl had almost no friends, was dangerously anorexic and barely literate. It's shocking to me now to remember how vulnerable I was before I joined the campaign. If I hadn't turned my attention outwards, if I hadn't found a way to make a difference, then my life would not have been filled with the incredible adventures I've enjoyed since. And I'm constantly thankful that I learned the power of happy heroism before it was too late.

Now I want to teach you that power, even if it's a long time since you felt the passion or purpose of a teenager.

Heroes in Waiting

I promise you that it's possible to feel better than you do right now. Too many of us today are suffering from an unhappy mess of low-level illnesses, unmanageable stress, loss of purpose and lack of confidence in how we look, in our relationships and in ourselves. We worry constantly about threats large and small, and struggle to feel hopeful about the future.

None of the fixes we're sold seem to work for long. From mindfulness to medication, every day a new diet, product or practice is launched to help us feel better. Each works for a while, yet somewhere down the road leaves us in our rut once again, wondering why we are so overwhelmed, tired and lost. And at our most vulnerable, sometimes we long for a hero to save us: someone to fix our own problems and the troubles we see around us; some strong, invincible, self-assured saviour who will make all the difference in our lives and even save the world.

And when we feel like that, we're right: the world does need more heroes – people who stand up and make a difference to others, who have the confidence and courage to change the world for the better.

But you're looking for a hero in the wrong places. No one else is coming to save you, because they don't have to. *You* are the hero you've been waiting for. You are the one who is going to change the world and, in the process, yourself. This is the handbook for you to discover this power you've always had. And I will show you how by turning outside of yourself, and trying to make the world a better place, your own life will begin to improve in unimaginable ways. You will discover a sense of control and self-confidence you never thought possible. You'll be happier, healthier and stronger, and you'll experience more joy every day. And you'll make an undeniable difference to the lives of others, helping to make our whole world a better place.

This book is your call to adventure. I'm asking you to change your life, and change it for the better. It won't be easy, but it will be wonderful. On each step of the journey I'll set out the actions and mindset shifts you'll work on, and the science of why those actions and mindsets will improve your health, resilience and relationships – and even help you live longer.

Every one of us can do this if we train ourselves to see the world differently and start doing something to improve it. Together we'll discover the evidence that making a difference in the world is the best way to make a difference to our own happiness. Remember: this isn't some airy-fairy new-age power, but instead the careful application of human determination and focus to achieve a beneficial outcome. Each part of happy heroism is based upon solid research in psychology, sociology and neuroscience. Yet the findings I'm using are too rarely plucked out of the pages of the scientific journals and put to work for our own happiness. So I've synthesised the research into the tools you need. And together we'll overcome the barriers (both internal and external) to fulfilling the goal that screenwriter Nora Ephron set for a group of young women: 'Above all, be the heroine of your life, not the victim.'

Our Superpower

Your first duty as a fledgling hero is to believe a better world is possible. You're going to read a lot about hope, positivity and optimism in this book. Because belief in the future is like a magic shield or superpower against all the worry and fear the world throws at you. It's also the only mindset that can change the world for the better.

Don't worry if you can't think of anything to feel hopeful about right now. This book is packed with surprising new data, technology and world-wide trends you might never have heard of. Things are better than you might think. And you have the power to make them even more amazing. The journey to happy heroism is going to be full of surprises, not least because it won't all be about you. While this is technically a 'self-help' book, the helping is going to work in the opposite direction. This book will boost your self-esteem and happiness – not by getting you to repeat mantras telling yourself that you're great, but by encouraging you to do great things in the world. You are going to change the lives of those around you, and far beyond, and in so doing you're going to feel better than you've ever felt before.

Living Proof

Over fifteen years ago, I co-founded Futerra, a company dedicated to finding pathways to a better future. In the early days, Futerra was just my friend Ed and me (along with the mice and pigeons which often invaded our office), working out of a badly converted birdseed warehouse in a dodgy part of south London. Everyone we worked with back then, even the good guys, considered the concept of people being positive about the future a weird one. Lots of them believed our little start-up wouldn't make it through its first few months.

Today, we're a global business with offices in London, New York, Stockholm and beyond. Every day I work with businesses, governments, charities and individuals to build a better future. It turns out that being positive was a pretty good business plan.

Over the years my work has meant that I've met hundreds of thousands of happy heroes. Many of them have achieved incredible things and are now living happy lives of purpose; and all of them started out just like you. Everything that I've learned at Futerra, be it in the boardroom or around kitchen tables, I use on myself as protection against the nasty mindsets that can drag people towards negativity or 'victimhood'. You'll find those skills within these pages, and they will help you to release yourself from stress and fear and into positivity and purpose.

We Need More Heroes

This book isn't just about you, because there is an entire world out there which also needs help right now. Thankfully, I know that if enough people adopt a happily heroic outlook on life, some of our biggest global problems might just begin to fade away.

Whole societies can benefit from the principles of happy heroism, in the same way that you and I can. Because societies in which most people feel optimistic about the future, and where they work together for real positive change, do better. That might sound obvious, but most of our societies today seem to have forgotten it, with discord and pessimism on the rise.

In times of collective threat (such as we face today), individual people's attitudes contribute to the difference between a creative or destructive result. From natural disasters to epidemics, and from economic shocks to conflicts, societies throughout history and across the world have faced difficult times. Some have risen to greater heights of peace and prosperity because of how they've dealt with their problems, while others have failed in the worst ways. In this book, we'll explore how individuals who feel positive and take positive action play as much a part in societal shifts as they do in individual lives. I will show you how, when citizens hold a collective, hopeful vision of their future and believe that together they can (with hard work) achieve that vision, the chances are that they will. This is the ultimate promise of happy heroism.

In stark contrast to positive societies, pessimistic cultures (which are internally divided and self-critical) are horribly vulnerable to even small shocks or upsets. Psychologists have known for some time that pessimistic people can struggle with crisis; now, sociologists are suggesting the same for whole societies that lack a positive vision. This is a big claim. But we'll see how staying positive and doing good isn't just good for you, it's good for all of us. And right now, we need something to turn our societies away from fear and back towards hope.

Our Shadow

Finding hope isn't easy when there are so many global perils that feel overwhelming, intractable and near impossible to address. From health crises to threats such as terrorism, feeling hopeful about the world right now is a big ask. And one of these problems is arguably even more complicated and overwhelming than everything else: climate change. I know that many people feel tempted to 'zone out' on issues like this. Climate change can be depressing and just so huge. And, bluntly, all the science and policy issues around it make it sound important, but tedious. Nevertheless, it's sneaking around in the back of your consciousness as a big shadowy threat. And according to recent surveys by the Pew Centre,[1] climate change is the most worrying issue globally, especially for young people.

It can feel almost trite to talk about 'positivity' and 'climate change' in the same sentence. But that's exactly what I'm going to do. Because it turns out that climate change is a perfect example of how acting to change the world comes with amazing benefits. That's why I've chosen climate change as the big 'shadow' we're going to confront in this book. Unlike so many of our other big threats, climate change isn't caused by ideology or one group fighting another, but by all 7 billion of us every single day. That makes it relevant everywhere in the world.

And when it comes to solving climate change, the benefits can be felt by both you personally and by the whole of society. Because almost everything we must do to solve climate change happens to

1. Jill Carle, 'Climate Change Seen as Top Global Threat', *Pew Research Center's Global Attitudes Project*, 14 July 2015 (web).

solve something else. Cutting down on air pollution will cure so many health problems, especially asthma in our children. Moving towards renewable energy will make countries energy-independent and avoid oil-induced conflicts and wars. Solar panels cut carbon emissions and, better than any other type of modern fuel, they bring light and hope to the poorest or most isolated people. Green energy isn't just green; it's now cheaper to source in many places in the world.

Building a new climate-friendly infrastructure is a massive task and will mean millions of new jobs and even entire new industries. In our own lives, we know that saving energy saves money. Electric cars cut oil use and cost much less to run (while accelerating like a jet). The UK's top medical journal, *The Lancet*, has even published a series of papers over the last decade proving that a 'low-meat and high-vegetable' diet would radically cut the carbon dioxide in our atmosphere. It also happens to be exactly the diet they recommend to protect your heart, slim your waistline and add years to your life. So from our health to our homes and jobs, taking positive action on climate change, be it large or small, seems to come with big practical paybacks.

We'll keep coming back to climate change in this book because it's the best example of my promise to you. The principles of happy heroism that I'm going to teach you apply to all our other problems, of course, but I've picked climate change as it's the toughest problem to solve, one that can make individual action feel irrelevant. But by the end of this book, you'll be wondering what you were so worried about. You'll be so focused on the rewards of action, and so convinced by that image of the amazing future we can reach, that climate change won't be scary any more. Nor will many of our other biggest global problems. They will become merely the push we need to build a better world. And every step you take to victory will come with personal rewards, both tangible and psychological.

The Hero's Journey

In 1949, an academic called Joseph Campbell wrote a book called *The*

Hero with a Thousand Faces. Within it he set out his conclusions from a meticulous review of mythology, fairy tales and long-held traditions of storytelling from different cultures across the world and throughout history. He analysed everything from Homer's voyages of Odysseus to the adventures of the Aztec mother goddess, and he discovered that the vast majority of our human stories follow the same basic structure, which he named the 'Hero's Journey'. The names and settings change, but the story is always the same – hence the single hero 'with a thousand faces'. Campbell makes a persuasive argument that the repetition of his hero's journey throughout history is no accident. This story structure is so common in our mythology because it maps the real psychological journey we must all go through to find our true nature (and to make a difference in our society). Today we keep on telling this old story because it resonates even in our modern world. The struggles and victories of Luke Skywalker or Dorothy in Oz follow the hero's journey exactly, and are so powerful because we see ourselves in them.

This book is your journey along this ancient pathway, past problems and through challenges, fighting a few dragons on your way.

Chapter 1, 'Your Adventure', is your first step on the road followed by heroes since the earliest times. You might need a little push to get started, so I'll reveal the powerful reasons for you to change, and the benefits you have waiting. We'll discover that the key to happy heroism is mental positivity and optimism, which then drives heroic action. I'll show how that works as a feedback loop, whereby your action makes you even more positive and optimistic. In mythology, guides and mentors traditionally give gifts to new heroes. My gift to you is a treasure map. This psychological plan of change is called the 'crisis curve' and it plots out the route to happiness (and the dangerous alternatives to avoid).

Every hero must face an enemy, which we'll meet in Chapter 2 – 'Enter the Dragon'. In stories, enemies can be anything from a great monster in the world to a darkness in the hero's own soul. But in every tale, only by confronting a shadow can the hero free their reward. Of all the potential threats we face today, I've chosen climate change to be the dragon of our story. This might seem like a rather large shadow for a new hero to defeat on their first try, but as you read through these pages, you'll acquire the tools that will unleash your positivity. And your training in happy heroism won't only help overcome that great threat, but will also help you to heal problems in your own community, your family and even in your heart.

But becoming a happy hero isn't easy, otherwise you'd already have done it. There are some nasty mindsets holding you back, and infecting whole societies, making us all vulnerable in the face of a crisis. Chapter 3, 'Past the Guards', will help you to jump clear of these mental obstacles and continue your adventure. And like everything else in this book, taking action to free yourself from negative outlooks will come with immediate rewards to your well-being.

In Chapter 4, 'Learning Heroism', you will truly start training to become a happy hero. You'll discover your own personalised list of heroic actions, tailored to your personality and preferences. You'll learn exercises that are proven to raise your self-esteem and plan ways to make changing the world both fulfilling and more fun than you expected. In most stories the hero makes some friends and allies on the way. So in this chapter we'll connect and plan to work together to change the world.

As you begin to feel the benefits of happy heroism and grow your confidence, things will start to feel amazing. But you're not free quite yet. Unleashing your power and positivity to change the world can provoke a backlash from others (or from inside yourself), as you will see in Chapter 5, 'Being Tested'. Truly accepting your power can be terrifying, and all your old neuroses and confidence killers will swarm up to drag you backwards. And sometimes making the world a better place can be thankless, or even draw criticism. These are tests every true hero must face, coming through them happier, stronger and more confident. I'll help you reposition your outlook to face the darkness and prevail.

In Chapter 6, 'Find the Secret', I'll show you a world you may not know exists. The world isn't only what we read about in the newspapers or the horrors we see on our screens. It's bigger, more complicated and a lot more beautiful than that. And there is a huge global shift already under way that you may never have heard of.

We'll explore the trends that will make being a happy hero a lot easier and ensure our world-changing actions are much more likely to succeed.

In Chapter 7, 'A Good Life', together we'll discover that there is a lot more to be hopeful about than you might expect. We'll take a tour of the world we're going to enjoy, should we choose to build it. By this point you'll have started to make small, positive actions, and you'll be experiencing the rewards. But now I'll ask more of you, and offer even more in return.

Finally, in Chapter 8, 'Our Future', we reach our destination. We'll look to the future and see how awesome things can be. And you'll make some lifelong commitments to being happier, more fulfilled and knowing that you truly matter in the world. You'll be a happy hero.

How to Use This Book

We're going to strike a balance from now on: we'll be wide-eyed optimists about a better future, and hard-nosed pragmatists about how to get there.

If you're already an optimist, you're going to roll your sleeves up and get to work on making things better, rather than just hoping they will be. You're going to exert yourself, see problems through common-sense-tinted glasses and plan realistically to face them square on.

If you're more of a pragmatist, you will need to pull back from the dangerous ledge of cynicism and negativity. Yes, you can use all that realism, but put it to work towards a bit of idealism. Let yourself believe that a better future is possible – damned hard to reach, maybe – but possible, none the less. And use that little flame of optimism to fuel your workmanlike ability to get things done.

All of us are unique, and starting our happy-hero journey from emotionally and physically different places. Some of us are already hopeful; others are struggling to think of anything to feel good about. Some might be leading movements to change the world already; others feel they make no impact on the world at all. What Joseph Campbell's book teaches us is that the hero has a thousand different faces. Throughout time and across the world we have told stories of heroes from every walk of life, and starting from the least heroic beginnings imaginable. So, this journey is for everyone, and especially for you.

Whether you're a natural optimist or a questioning realist, this book opens the door to a kind of life that we all too rarely let ourselves believe is possible. We're going to imagine a future for each other and ourselves in which, with hard work, things can be so much better than they are today, with the added bonus that working to make that vision a reality comes with immediate, built-in personal rewards: each and every one of us can be a happy hero and start feeling good by doing good.

We've got a world to save; capes and masks are optional.

1

Your Adventure

a The only thing we have to fear is fear itself.

—Franklin D. Roosevelt

Your adventure starts here. Right now, you are a hero in training and taking your first steps in a journey to change yourself, and change the whole world. Take a deep breath and whisper to yourself: 'I am a hero.' With your out-breath a little tension will be released and hopefully a little excitement will take its place.

That's the happy-hero 'feedback loop' that you're starting to feel, designed to make you feel great by doing good:

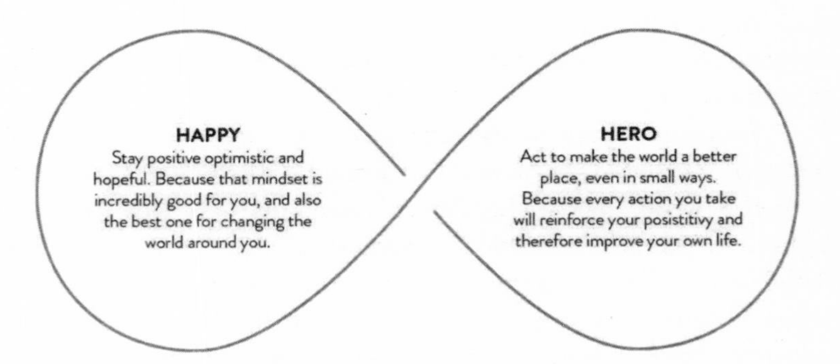

Of course, like many things, this is easy to write down, but rather harder to do. But we'll work on it together, step by step. You'll learn new skills, decide your actions and avoid some pitfalls and dangers along the way to happy heroism. And I won't just tell you *what* to do; I'll prove to you *why* it is worth doing.

The Rewards of Happiness

When a 99-year-old nun called Sister Mary said, 'Sign me up,' to a group of researchers, she changed the future of psychology. Born in 1892, when Victoria was still queen of England, by 1990 Sister Mary had been a nun for nearly 80 years and a teacher for most of them. Throughout her life, she was dedicated to service and helping others. Perhaps it's unsurprising, then, that she was the first of a group of elderly nuns to agree when scientists from the University of Kentucky asked for volunteers for research on ageing.

Over 600 Catholic nuns across the US joined her to have their health and attitudes monitored over decades, in what became arguably the most famous scientific study on the power of positivity. Researchers were very excited because nuns make perfect test subjects: they eat the same things, work together, sleep at set times, don't smoke or drink and rarely travel. Because their lifestyles are so similar, other factors which might affect their health and longevity can be more easily spotted. The study ran for over 20 years, starting when many of the nuns were already in their fifties or older. But because they had all written a brief 'application statement' of their feelings on entering their convents, evidence on their mental states was available from as far back as the 1930s.

The researchers went through each one of these historical statements and counted the positive or negative words and phrases the nuns had written about themselves, sometimes over half a century before. Words like 'gratitude', 'happiness', 'joy', 'hope', 'love' and 'relief' were coded as positive. Words associated with anger, contempt, disgust, disinterest, fear, sadness and shame were marked as negative. The health and well-being of the nuns were then monitored as they aged. Many of the women knew they would probably pass away during the study, and they dedicated their bodies to science.

The conclusions of the 'Nun Study', as it became known, were startling. The researchers found that the most positive and optimistic nuns lived for nearly a decade longer than their more neutral or pessimistic colleagues. This was impressive enough, but the study also revealed that the positive nuns suffered fewer symptoms of dementia – something that was attributed not to their lifestyle choices, which were all very similar, but to their positive emotions. Sister Mary herself had been one of the most positive and active of the nuns studied. After she passed away, early in the study, it was discovered that her brain was riddled with the lesions and plaques that doctors associate with Alzheimer's. Despite this, she had never shown any symptoms and scored highly in memory tests, even when over 100 years of age. Her longevity and mental acuity seemed to have been significantly affected by her positive attitude, compared to the more downbeat sisters.

When the results of the 'positive nuns' research were published, they caused a storm in psychology and neuroscience that has yet to quieten.[1] Many of us have heard similar stories about the transformative power of positivity. A growing body of research is proving the incredible benefits of optimism: from transforming your health, wealth and happiness, to improving your love life, friendships and earning potential.

Except that there is a catch. We are not all 'happy nuns'. Right now, you might not feel all that positive, happy or heroic. You might be the opposite. Positivity doesn't have a switch you can just flick on, and words like 'stressed', 'worried' and 'overwhelmed' might more accurately describe your emotional state. Feeling hopeful in the world today can be incredibly hard. We're becoming less trusting of our neighbours and more concerned about threats lurking in our communities, our food and our economy. Almost every society or nation seems beset by complex and seemingly unresolvable challenges and deepening divisions. Even our planet – our air and water – is under threat from giant monsters like climate change. Surveys show that people, and especially those who live in developed economies, are feeling increasingly worried about their own prospects and progressively less hopeful that their futures will be positive.[2] It seems that

1. David A. Snowdon, 'Aging and Alzheimer's Disease: Lessons from the Nun Study', *The Gerontologist*, 37.2 (1997): 150–6.

2. Pew Research Center's Global Attitudes Project, *Pew Research Center's Global Attitudes Project RSS*, n.p., 30 March 2017.

just as psychology is proving the transformative benefits of positivity, hope is becoming harder to find.

The Rewards of Heroism

When I think about overcoming barriers to feeling positive, I'm often reminded of Ebenezer Scrooge from Charles Dickens's *A Christmas Carol*, who, after his famous night of ghosts and guilt, awakens with a new attitude. But it's not until he acts on it, changing the lives of Tiny Tim and the others around him, that he truly starts to feel happy himself. Only through taking action does Scrooge become physically well and practically effervescent, until he is 'as good a man, as the good old city knew, or any other good old city, town, or borough, in the good old world'. Scrooge teaches us that optimism and positivity are very hard to generate 'from the inside'. Instead, the very best way to *feel* positive is to *do* something positive.

That's how the happy-hero feedback loop works. Feeling good can be hard, but doing good is very good for you. And then feeling happy will come as a direct result of acting heroically, even in small ways. Both the 'happy' and the 'hero' parts of the formula come with their own rewards. And because the happy part – optimism, positivity and hope – can be so hard to generate by itself, the hero part – making a difference – sometimes comes first. Put simply, doing good feels good. So, rather than waiting to feel hopeful, or looking to others to fix the world's problems, the very best thing we can do is to start building a better future ourselves.

In nearly 20 years of leading pro-social and environmental campaigns through my company Futerra, I've seen this effect in action many times over. Scientists are now researching this neurological 'do-good dividend' that we can all enjoy by taking positive action. If you don't feel positive, then start doing positive things and your feelings will catch up.

Dr Stephen G. Post is one of the world's leading experts in this emerging field of 'give and thou shalt receive'. His team measured the 'helper's high' that we can all experience through taking positive action and found that two-thirds of the people he studied felt a positive physical sensation from helping, while approximately half said they actually felt 'high'. Others felt stronger and more energetic, warmer and calmer. For a lucky 13 per cent of people, the act of helping others even relieved their own physical aches and pains.[3]

Particularly generous acts of goodness, like volunteering your time, have been proven to deliver especially big paybacks. Volunteering makes you happier, raises your well-being and can even reduce depression. Importantly, this isn't just a 'perceived' benefit: the well-being you experience from doing good measurably affects your brain chemistry. When you act to help others or make a difference, your brain produces its own healthy version of heroin, called endorphins. The helper's high is exactly that: a totally natural buzz generated by your own brain. That's what I was feeling when I climbed those bricks to celebrate our win against nuclear dumping. And this is what I experience every day in the work that I do.

The simple truth is that the best way to feel better is to make the world a better place. And a lot of people are already in on this secret. As a student studying mathematics at Manchester University in 2009, Ed Broni-Mensah decided to start a harsh fitness regime, which promised he would 'get ripped in ninety days'. In addition to long runs and workouts the plan required him to drink over 4 litres of water each day. To hit that target, Ed had to keep refilling his water bottle, even while out on a gruelling run. But many of the shops and cafés he stopped at to ask for a top-up seemed confused or downright unwelcoming. That awkwardness led Ed to think about how his own parents in Ghana had struggled to find clean water as children. And he had a brainwave about how to help. The result? Hundreds of shops and restaurants across the country today have agreed to fill up his reusable GiveMeTap bottles for free. Every GiveMeTap bottle purchased gives another person in Africa five years of clean water access through the installation of water pumps. 'I was on a fitness programme and trying to get a six-pack before I was 25,' says Ed. 'Who would guess that would eventually help me build a successful business

3. Stephen G. Post, 'Altruism, Happiness, and Health: It's Good to Be Good', *International Journal of Behavioral Medicine*, 12.2 (2005): 66–77.

and even change lives?' Ed is a true happy hero (and I suspect he's got the six-pack, too). And he is only one of the millions of people already discovering the benefits of positivity and action.

Dr David R. Hamilton, author of *Why Kindness Is Good for You*, decided to test whether helping could even extend your life. He conducted a study of 846 people over the age of 65, who were interviewed about the stressful events they had experienced over the previous year (like bereavement, loss of income or illness).[4] His team also asked how often the interviewees helped their friends or family members by providing lifts, doing errands, shopping, housework or providing childcare. The researchers already knew that when older people experience a stressful event, it can increase their risk of mortality over the following five years. But being a helpful person breaks that dangerous link. Dr Hamilton's team found that the helpful people had greater resilience and were statistically more likely to survive any stressful experiences. The similarities to the nun study are important. The optimistic and positive nuns also lived longer (and were, anecdotally, also eager to be 'of service' to others). So just imagine the feedback-loop benefits of putting the optimism rewards together with the helper's high.

Older people aren't the only ones who experience these rewards of virtue. In the 1990s, the University of Miami investigated the special characteristics of people who had survived AIDS over the long term. They discovered that a key factor was that they were 'more likely to help others' who had HIV.[5] Because even if you're ill yourself, simply helping others can measurably boost your own immune system.

4. Michael J. Poulin, Stephanie L. Brown, Amanda J. Dillard and Dylan M. Smith, 'Giving to Others and the Association Between Stress and Mortality', *American Journal of Public Health*, 103.9 (2013): 1649–55.

5. Allen M. Omoto and Mark Snyder, 'Sustained Helping Without Obligation: Motivation, Longevity of Service, and Perceived Attitude Change Among AIDS Volunteers', *Journal of Personality and Social Psychology*, 68.4 (1995): 671–86.

Collective Gifts

The feedback loop between heroism and your own happiness can transform your life, and I hope that it will. But that's only half my formula. The other half is not about you alone, but about all of us. Because it's not only individuals who can be changed by happy heroism. Whole societies can have an underlying zeitgeist or collective unconscious. And the way we talk about our prospects as a country or community can subtly (or sometimes quite obviously) affect how we all act.

That's why your attitude about the world is important, for you and for all of us. Because your positivity and optimism won't only affect your own life, it could affect the lives we'll all get to lead. The ripples of your happy heroism will be felt throughout society. And if enough of us start feeling optimistic about our future (and act optimistically), then a better future is exactly what we'll get. That's why I'm here to prove to you that tomorrow can be better than today.

Thankfully, as well as researching the psychology of happy heroism, I've also spent two decades searching out the shifts towards a better world that are already happening across the globe. And I know that the next few decades could be incredible, if we decide to make them so. We will revolutionise our energy systems and break through the glass ceiling that keeps us trapped in methods of manufacture that a medieval farmer might recognise. Our cities will be transformed from life-sucking warrens of bad food, bad air and stress into smart and beautiful places where kids will enjoy growing up. We're not only going to feed billions of people but we're going to feed them well, the obese and the starving at either end of the spectrum pulled into a healthy middle ground. We're all going to read, write and learn. Our engineers, scientists and innovators are going to play with getting us to the stars, connecting us through new technologies, extending our lives and surrounding us with gizmos that make life extraordinary. And all this won't be for only the privileged 1 per cent, but for all of us. It's going to be science fiction, minus the fiction. You're also going to change for the better. You'll feel proud of yourself and know you're doing the right thing with your life. You'll worry less and hope more. You'll look forward to tomorrow. You'll be healthier and safer, have more time, closer relationships, sleep better and enjoy yourself more. Even your love life is going to improve (and I have the science to prove it). If you struggle to believe that right now, it's my job to make sure you do by the end of this book. Because being able to see and feel this positive future is your secret weapon against despair, apathy and anger. And it's the best way to avoid worries becoming self-fulfilling prophecies.

Truly believing this positive vision is heroic, because it's all too easy to imagine darker scenarios, especially when it comes to huge global problems like climate change. That dark vision of global warming is of wild weather, melting ice caps, homes and crops swept away by floods, hurricanes, wildfires and parched earth; of wars over resources, with draconian governments rationing your food, energy and travel, and creating masses of huddled refugees scourged by unforgiving storms and droughts.

This dystopian picture is becoming all too familiar. So much so that it takes strength of will to challenge it. It's almost as if we enjoy the threat of the horrors and darkness about to fall upon us. Our media certainly does. But if we look carefully, there is always someone offering light amid the gloom.

The Shoulders of Giants

Imagine, for a moment, that you are standing on the grand marble steps of the Lincoln Memorial in Washington DC. It's a hot August day in 1963. The largest crowd ever gathered in the capital city is fuelling the noise and heat. Facing you is a sea of humanity so large that you can't see where the crowd ends. And every single one of those faces is watching you and waiting for you to speak.

What will you say?

It would be so easy to speak in anger. A speech bursting with fury and spite would be justified, particularly considering what you, and many of those thousands of waiting people, have been through. You've been fighting a long harsh battle against injustice, and sometimes it has felt like a long defeat. Your own home has been bombed and your family has been persecuted. Every phone call you make is tapped and jail has become all too familiar. The anger and frustration of your supporters is tangible. Blood has already been spilled, including your own. Even your most peaceful followers now suspect that civil war is the only answer. Real, bloody, mortal fighting has begun. Terror may be the only way forward.

What will you say?

'I have a dream today.'

Dr Martin Luther King Jr. chose hope over fear when standing on those steps. He was able to hold onto a positive vision of what was possible, even in the face of horrible injustice and fear. And his positivity still resonates throughout our culture all these decades later. Over the course of history, so many of our greatest heroes seem to have known intuitively something that has taken me years of research and experience to realise: hope works.

What would the world look like today if Dr King had spoken in anger rather than hope? Or if Mahatma Gandhi had called for violence rather than positive action?

Unfortunately, it's not that hard to imagine. We have too many examples of what happens to a society when furious despots and demagogues threaten fear and destruction rather than offering hope and positivity. When people follow fear and threat, the pathway rarely leads to progress. From Winston Churchill to Nelson Mandela, our greatest leaders have always grasped the potential of the hopeful positive. They didn't need sociological studies to tell them that morale matters, because they lived and breathed it.

These heroes all fought against the great horrors of their times. Each of them led their people with hope and a steely optimism to confront the great 'shadows' of racism, fascism and imperialism. Our greatest heroes before and since have had a similar ability to see past threats to a better world beyond.

And now it's your turn, because today we need millions of visionaries who believe a better world is possible, and are prepared to work to achieve it. Not least because the benefit of believing that is a reward in itself.

Guards at the Gate

Much of the research I'll explore in this book has already become mainstream. But if you're a pragmatist, you might now be asking: 'Well, if this effect is so powerful, why isn't everyone already trying happy heroism? Why aren't doctors prescribing volunteering or schools teaching positivity?'

Thankfully, a few already are, but it can feel like pushing against the tide. It can be incredibly hard to stay positive, optimistic and helpful, especially in the modern world. Because there are guards blocking your transformation. Much of our media acts as a brake on your happiness. Too much of the news and advertising we watch subtly torments us. The messages strip us of our right to be the heroes of our lives and instead tell us we are victims, beset by unimaginable dangers we can't control. The front pages of our newspapers scream constant daily threats, and the adverts promise to save us from imperfections we didn't know we had. All this conspires to make 'them', be they companies or politicians, the all-powerful ones and 'us' the powerless who must wait for the next product or policy which might save us. No wonder my Bedfordshire neighbours looked a little puzzled by their victory against a big company. It's not supposed to work that way around.

Perhaps the worst offenders in promoting this 'self-victimisation' are in the very industry many of us turn to for help. This is essentially a self-help book promising that you can change your life by changing the world. But most self-help books encourage their readers to turn inwards and try to fix themselves, while ignoring the needs of others. And the self-help industry is self-sustaining because, for too many of us, that approach simply doesn't work. We buy one book hoping it will make us feel better, look good, find a purpose and be happy, then turn to another when it doesn't work. But I believe these books are teaching us to look in the wrong direction. Rather than looking inwards, we should look outwards at the world, because the real paybacks come when we start trying to fix what we see around us, rather than becoming ever more obsessed with ourselves.

To help you make this massive change in your outlook and

actions I have tools, training and gifts to share, the first of which is a map of what you're likely to face as you become a happy hero.

The Map

In stories, the hero always faces a series of tests, a journey with choices, allies and enemies along the way. They follow a long path before they walk off happily into the sunset. This structure feels right to us because it matches the way in which real-life crises are faced and solved. In psychology, this journey is called the 'crisis curve', and from our own personal crisis to big, global problems like climate change the curve is surprisingly consistent.

For us individually, the crisis curve plots the psychological steps through some of the biggest moments of challenge and doubt we can face. And it's comforting to know that in many cases, if you follow the right path through the curve, you can come out better than when you started. Entire societies and cultures have also faced the curve, passing through periods of dramatic change on the way to an outcome that was almost unimaginable at the start. For both individuals and societies, the curve always means change: on one side is the world we know; on the other is a world we can't yet imagine. A lot of factors collide, and things that have always been true stop being so. New truths are found.

The crisis curve isn't a new idea; it can be found in the stories of individuals, communities and whole civilisations throughout history. Historians call the periods when societies pass through the curve 'axial ages', revolution eras and renaissances. For the happy hero, all this research is fantastic news because it means that the crisis curve has already been carefully mapped, with 'here be gold' and 'here be monsters' helpfully plotted. If you've ever faced a crisis of your own, then you'll probably recognise parts of this as we delve into it. Hopefully, your personal crisis curve was navigable and you exited in better shape than you entered. But it isn't always fun when you're stuck in the middle of the curve itself.

When I was a young girl, my family hit a crisis curve that almost chewed us up. The crisis began when my father fell off the scaffolding where he was working as a builder. He fell six floors down from a wooden platform that was fit only for firewood. My dad is from a long line of Irish workmen who, as he says himself, were 'bred for strong backs and digging holes'. But his Irish strength couldn't save him that day. Broken bones and torn skin heal; three slipped discs and two crushed vertebrae don't. That was it. My father, the work-horse – the man who could lift me with one hand – was now broken, with the prognosis that he would never walk properly again. It was disastrous, heartrending and terrifying for a family who relied on his wages. But Dad's plight wasn't totally unfamiliar to my mother, who already had one cripple in the house. A year earlier, her very gaunt and shy daughter had performed in a school gymnastics display. Later that night, she (well, I) had started screaming with pain. I'd dislocated my hip joint and had a dark stain of internal bleeding. Months later, I still couldn't walk or attend school, and now my father's crutches lay alongside my wheelchair in our tiny council house.

I can't imagine what that winter was like for my mother, living on meagre government handouts and trying to raise two other daughters while she planned a life of caring for her broken husband and lame child.

Then things got even worse. The social housing we lived in was one in a row of houses that were home to drug users, criminals and one very violent woman. One night, this woman took affront to something my mother had said. She broke in, grabbed my mum by her hair and tried to beat her head against our oven. I was the only person nearby and struggled to push her off. As fast as she had arrived, and with a final scream of rage, she left, but not before she'd pulled out clumps of my mother's hair, leaving her shaking with horror on the floor.

That was our darkest moment. But it was also a turning point for us all. That was the day my mother decided our lives were going to change. She'd hit the worst part of the crisis curve – we all had – and things were either going to spiral downwards into violence, shame and break-up or our family was going to transform itself beyond recognition. My father and I were going to walk again; my mother's plan didn't allow for anything else. Dad was going to retrain for a job that made proper money and used his passions rather than his Irish back. I was going back to school, and maybe even on to university (something no one in our family had ever done). We were going to move out of the council estate.

The only way to drag ourselves out of that pit was to shoot for the stars. Halfway wouldn't do it; back to square one would be a disaster. So shoot for the stars we did. Dad trained as a stonemason and worked on the cathedrals and ancient monuments of England, and Mum went to college to train as a schoolteacher. My sisters and I went to university or learned a trade. I won't pretend it was an easy journey, and my father never fully recovered from his injuries, but we worked together and we worked hard. We never let doubt or apathy claim us.

A few years ago, my parents retired to a sprawling farmhouse in the Italian countryside with a little vineyard on the side. Visited in the sun by their daughters and grandchildren, they've created a better picture than anyone could have imagined (except for my mum, of course).

Only the iron-clad hope my mother discovered was able to save my family. And the same type of hard-working hope is desperately needed today for our global family of humanity. Our worldwide neighbourhood is getting tougher, and we've got to drag ourselves, our families and all our billions of neighbours out of it and into the sunshine.

There are 'big heroes', like firefighters, who do extraordinary things every day. But there is also a different kind of heroism, one that can be found in kitchens, offices and schools, if you look hard enough. These everyday heroes can also change the world. And their rewards come as a result of them changing their mindset in order to change their actions and change the world. Most of this book is dedicated to making that happen. But the crisis curve also teaches us that there are some unpleasant alternatives to being a hero. So familiarise yourself with the curve to map your hero's journey through it.

Meet the Crisis Curve

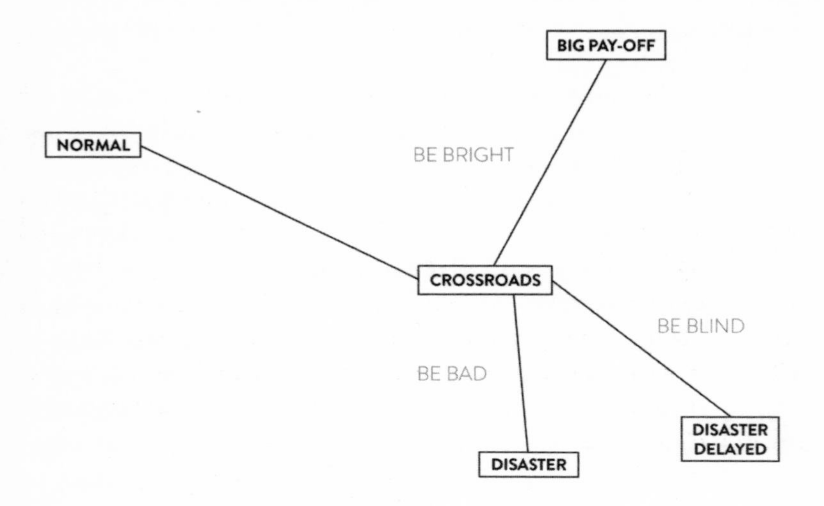

Historians, political scientists, psychologists and therapists alike have researched, argued about and picked apart this curve. Their work has given us some basic signposts and directions along the way. We're going to need every one of their hints and hard-learned lessons to see us safely through. Their directions are easy to understand, if not always simple to follow.

Normal

A crisis always starts with some small shifts in 'normal'. A tiny ember burns, the sky fills with cloud, a few pebbles fall…

For individuals, a crisis might start when damaging behaviours (like heavy drinking) that have slowly built up suddenly start causing real and visible problems. On a more global scale, with something like climate change, we can track those little pebbles falling from a long way off. We've been burning up carbon for centuries but it's taken a lot of pebbles and a few rocks to fall before we've started to notice anything. The signs of wider change and a sort of 'mass crisis' even beyond the climate aren't hard to spot. Many of us already feel the pull of this curve, and are aware that it's getting stronger.

We've noticed, and now we need to decide what to do about it.

Crisis Grows

One of my favourite Albert Einstein quotes is his definition of insanity, which he says is 'doing the same thing over and over again and expecting different results'.

As individuals or societies head towards a defining crisis point, which I call the crossroads, things can look a little crazy. More and more people become aware of the crisis, talk about it, argue about it and worry and worry and worry. But they don't *do* much differently. This is a familiar stage in crisis theory, especially for individuals. In Chapter 5 we'll look at all the 'maladaptations' and avoidance tactics we use when we're in this situation. But the signs of intensifying crisis are easy to spot:

- Growing anxiety: people begin feeling fretful and ineffectual; individuals and whole governments seem chaotic and uncoordinated. Everyone feels 'at sea' and 'lost'.
- More frustration: we keep trying the same old things and feel increasingly irritated when they don't work.
- Anger: some people get defensive and blame others or deny the problem.

Sound familiar? These are the symptoms of any crisis, be it personal or societal.

Crossroads

The word 'crisis' itself comes from the ancient Greek word '*krisis*', which means a decision or turning point. When the curve hits the 'crossroads', everything has built up and now something's got to give. In the academic research on crisis these are called 'transcrisis points' or 'axial moments'. They happen to individuals, groups and whole societies. In his book *The Tipping Point*, Malcolm Gladwell said: 'Look at the world around you. It may seem like an immovable, implacable place. It is not. With the slightest push – in just the right place – it can be tipped.'

But I want to adapt that idea a little to allow for the fact that things can 'tip' in different directions. It's not as simple as a balance eventually being tipped in one direction or another. For societies facing a crisis point, it is more like climbing a long road and then reaching a fork. We get a choice about which way things will tip.

Some societies still consider crossroads to be almost magic. Today you might find statues, crucifixes or shrines at junctions. The Romans built altars at them, and in medieval Britain executed criminals were buried there. Modern physics is even delving into the theoretical crossroads between different dimensions. Human beings have always known that decision moments are important, and that one decision can take you to a radically different destination. That's why crossroads have a special status in our literature and mythology.

Individuals can stand at psychological crossroads for a few moments, or can struggle to decide their next steps for years. And there is always a mindset shift before people take a step beyond their crossroads. We are either able to move past our crisis mentally, reset our attitudes and improve our lives, or we succumb to it, lacking the will for change. To those watching, it may seem obvious what we need to do, but until we've seen our own path out, they can't help us. Happy heroism is the mindset that serves us best when we face a crisis. It accepts the possibility of a better future, and puts us in service to that purpose. Attain that mindset and the right actions will follow. As you read through this book, that mindset will slowly develop, until you can pass any crisis you meet.

And the same principles apply to the crisis our entire society faces. Right now, we're shuffling closer to a big crossroads in terms of climate change. We're not quite there yet, because we're not fully exhibiting the signs of a society at the very threshold of change, but we're getting very close. And the happy heroes have already decided their direction and are striding up the brighter path. We'll know our entire societies are at the crossroads when people display what the psychologists call 'openness'. Openness is when you know you must make a decision, when you accept that things are going to change, and so your creative ideas and solutions suddenly start spilling out. Psychologists have learned how to spot a patient who is ready to change, and their definitions[6] are helpful for any crisis management. We'll know our collective feet are unambiguously standing at the crossroads when we all feel:

- Openness: when we have maximum awareness and interest in the crisis, looking for lots of ideas, being open and suggestible to both good (and bad) advice.
- Energy: when we put all our focus on emergency methods or creative, novel solutions to the problem, trying everything and agreeing on nothing.

Some might argue that we've already hit this point in our climate crisis, but I suspect there's a little more to come (or we need to stand at the crossroads a little longer to fully experience it). Being fully there will feel like a bizarre mixture of panic and calm, frenzy and reflection, everywhere in the world.

But we do have some sociological blueprints of the direction we should take next because humanity has already passed through ages when the pressure of a societal crossroads unleashed an overflowing pot of progress and creativity. The German philosopher Karl Jaspers coined the term 'axial ages' to describe these periods of history, when societies seem to take a big jump forward. He realised that an unusually well-travelled person in the fifth century BC could have conceivably met Confucius, Lao-Tze, the Buddha, Zoroaster and Socrates over the course of a 70-year lifetime, because within a single century Socrates was founding philosophy in ancient Greece, the Buddha was experiencing enlightenment in India, Confucius was laying laws in China, and the foundations of Judaism were established. A century might sound like a long time, but after thousands of years of relative stability, the whole modern basis of society suddenly arose. We've been following the path set at that particular crossroads for millennia since.

The Renaissance, Enlightenment and Industrial Revolution have also been described as 'axial ages': times of change so pivotal that it's impossible to imagine how history would have progressed without

6. Robin Davidson, 'Can Psychology Make Sense of Change?' Chapter 4, in Griffith Edwards and Malcolm Harold Lader (Eds), *Addiction: Processes of Change* (Oxford: Oxford University Press, 1994).

them. These periods are both hugely destructive as well as creative. Many old ways of thinking and old systems of technology and organisation are simply swept away, to be replaced entirely by new ones. They aren't great times to be afraid of change. The transition isn't always comfortable, but humanity's lot can be hugely improved by it.

New ideas abound at crossroads, and not all of them are good. Just as we have precedents for taking the right road out, we also know that sometimes societies take the wrong one. Germany being lured into Nazism after the First World War or the fall of the Roman Empire offer important lessons in the paths to avoid. You're not guaranteed a renaissance when your society hits a crisis curve. There are rules for making the right choice, whether as one person or an entire civilisation. Both our collective history and individual psychology agree that how you think will dictate what you do. And hard experience shows that at a crossroads there are only three directions to choose:

Be Bad

Being bad is the worst and most foolish path. It means pretending there isn't a crossroads, or saying we're doomed to walk down only one pathway. In the context of climate change, the bad mindset right now is either denial or doom. They might sound different, but they are both trying to drive us down the same terrible route. And it's a path with no rewards; all you are left with is a last-ditch fight to survive a certain disaster. This path should have a big 'Beware: Dead End Ahead' sign hanging beside it.

Be Blind

Being blind in this context means deliberately squeezing your eyes shut when you can actually see. It means hoping to reach the destination of one path, but by walking down a different one; asking for the big reward without doing any of the things guaranteed to deliver it. We've all done this when trying to put off a difficult decision or when hoping that things will just work themselves out. For climate change this means accepting the reality of the problem, but not what we need to do about it – trying the old solutions to the new problem. The blind mindset is technically referred to as 'maladaptation', and right now there's a lot of it about. We don't want to make a blind choice at this crossroads because the destination of that path is delayed disaster, but disaster nevertheless.

Be Bright

This is the road to major payback. Take this path and we'll all change – a lot. But every change will come with its own reward. It's bright to choose your path at the crossroads based on the destination you want to reach. It's bright to think positively and hopefully when you stride out along it. It's bright to join together with others when you travel. And it's bright to try new things and explore possibilities. This is the happy-hero pathway, and many are already taking it. It's the smartest choice, but not always the easiest, because it means radical change. But right now, change seems inevitable anyway; too much has already happened. It's up to us either to be swept along in the change, or to direct it towards the outcome we want.

Because bright knows where it's going.

*

The Story of a Happy Hero

'I got upset at school today,' Ben said.

Like any mum, Jane usually loved the few minutes just chatting with her son before she turned out his light. But as she put away the book they'd been reading, he looked up at her with a serious expression on his usually cheeky face.

Jane slowly sat down on the edge of the bed, giving Ben her full attention and trying to radiate a calm warmth as he went on. 'We watched a film about climate change in Mr Ackers's class,' Ben said. 'It was made for kids and had cartoons and that. But, well, everything was getting worse, with storms and ice melting and polar bears starving and people not being able to grow food.' He struggled to express the scale of the problems he'd seen. 'Well, it was all horrible, really; some of the kids were really scared and one girl cried.' He didn't say any more and just looked down, biting his lip as he did when worried or concentrating.

Jane took a deep breath and gave her son's leg a little squeeze. 'I'm sorry, Ben,' she said. 'They really shouldn't show things like that to kids.' She tried to add a note of adult assurance to her voice. 'But you don't need to worry about things like that yet, and anyway, they'll have sorted it all out by the time you've grown up.' Ben didn't say anything else, and as it was getting late Jane just kissed his forehead and went through the ritual of light switches and goodnight wishes.

Downstairs she heard Chris watching the news but decided she simply couldn't face hearing about the latest bombings, crises or horrors. Anyway, she was still worried about Ben, so she sat down at the kitchen table with her tablet to check her favourite parenting website. She wanted to see if anyone else had dealt with a similarly worried child. She was a little put out the school had scared the children like that, and without even a note sent home about it. Online she found a lot of other parents commenting on a thread about climate-change lessons:

> My six-year-old daughter asked me about Arctic ice melt-

> ing today. I thought she was worried about the penguins (she loves them), so I told her they would be fine. But she said, 'There aren't any penguins at the Arctic, Mummy, only the Antarctic.' Mummy not feeling very smart right now!
>
> Mum of two girls

> The whole climate change stuff is too much for kids – save that for later!
>
> Mum of darling son

> Who the hell knows what to say to a thing like that anyway?
>
> Dad of three

Most felt the same way as she did, and shared ideas about how to comfort kids. Others seemed angry about climate change being taught at all, calling it 'political correctness' and not proper science. Their comments incited responses from others equally angry about 'the future we're leaving our kids'. Some of the posts on both sides had got quite nasty.

Jane carefully avoided those conversations and posted her own response about what she'd said to Ben, but admitting that 'it hadn't felt like enough'. And then she added:

> As he gets older he'll find out more and more about things like this – all the bad things in the world – but what am I supposed to say to him about all that, when I don't even know what to do myself?
>
> Mum of dearest son

She closed her tablet and thought about going for a run or trying to cook something. She'd promised herself that she'd try to be a bit healthier now that Ben was getting older. But all she wanted to do was snuggle on the sofa with her husband and order pizza again, carefully avoiding watching the news. Her self-help books talked about making 'lifestyle commitments', and she kept seeing pictures of super-skinny mums online with 'What's your excuse?' plastered over their abs. But right now she felt more like crying than crunching. She opened her tablet again to order a takeaway and noticed a new reply to her earlier post. And it wasn't like the responses she normally saw on the site:

> Your son is a hero! And he's just given you the most wonderful gift. He's invited you on an adventure. And it's one that might just change your life, and his too. Are you willing to take the first step?
>
> The Godmother

She was surprised. Sometimes other parents on the site had helped to change her mind about problems she'd faced. But this was the strangest response she'd ever had. For a moment she considered shooting back a cutting reply about parenting already being enough of an adventure, thank you. But perhaps because of how low she was feeling, or because she was warmed by the thought of Ben being a hero, she wrote back instead: 'If it's good for my son, then I guess I'm in…'

2

Enter the Dragon

First they ignore you, then they laugh at you, then they fight you, then you win.

—Mahatma Gandhi

I hope you're beginning to feel a little heroic and perhaps even experiencing a few flutters of happiness at the idea of making a difference in the world. In Chapter 3 we will fan those little flames of happy heroism and train you to really start changing your life. But first I need to turn you outside of yourself to face the world. And that might take some doing if you've been focused on your problems for too long. But happy heroes change the world first, and themselves as a result.

One of the reasons I chose climate change as the great enemy in this hero's journey is because it's so big, so complex and so outside the normality of our lives. That makes it the perfect issue to pull us out of our little personal bubble and into the big, wide world.

I want to properly introduce the dragon we need to slay and the secret of how to slay it. And while doing so remind you that you are so very powerful that you actually have the ability to make a difference even on this scale.

A Sleeping Dragon

People have long suspected that we might be able to change the weather. The ancient Greeks worried that cutting down forests might affect rain in pastures (which on a large scale it can). But most of our weather is very specific and very local. Our planet gets lots of changeable weather from moment to moment. There can be a 'once-in-a-lifetime' flood in New York or a 'freak' drought in Sydney on the same day. But our 'climate' is different to our 'weather'. Our climate is the overall temperature and atmospheric systems measured over very long time periods, and big changes to it are very rare. As Mark Twain put it: 'Climate is what we expect, weather is what we get.' Predicting the weather can be hard, but predicting the climate used to be very easy: you might not know what tomorrow's temperature would be, but you did know that winter would be colder and summer hotter.

While a huge change in weather of several degrees between one day and the next might only be a problem if you forget your coat, tiny changes of just a few degrees in the global climate over time will have a monumental impact on our weather systems. Think of weather as a collection of objects sitting on a table: they might roll around a bit, but the table remains steady underneath. Our climate is the steady table, but if you shave even a tiny amount off one leg, then suddenly things become very unstable on the tabletop.

People in Greenhouses Shouldn't Throw Stones

People have always been more interested in the things on the table (the weather) rather than the table itself (the climate). It wasn't until the 19th century that scientists stopped checking out of the window and started thinking about the planet's climate as a whole.

In 1827 a French 'gentleman-scientist' called Jean-Baptiste Joseph Fourier wondered why the earth's atmosphere was so warm, considering it travels about in the freezing vacuum of space. It seemed quite weird to him that it's so nice down here, and so cold up there. He suggested that something about the earth's atmosphere must be trapping the sun's heat close enough to all the trees, oceans and people to make life liveable. He compared this heat-trapping effect to that of a greenhouse. (Gentleman-scientists of the early 19th century often kept greenhouses in their well-manicured gardens to protect delicate plants from the cold European weather.) This is where we get the term 'greenhouse effect' from, and it's a very good thing in the right dose, because we need some stable carbon dioxide in our atmosphere to trap some warmth down here. And for a very long time we had the perfect amount. But then things changed.

Seventy years after Fourier was inspired by a garden greenhouse, a superbly moustachioed Swedish physicist named Svante August Arrhenius began to worry that the windows of the global greenhouse were getting too thick. He suggested that the carbon-dioxide emissions from the burning of coal (used in steam trains and cotton mills back then) would build up in that greenhouse and warm the planet uncomfortably.

This is what we mean by global warming, and people have known about it for over a century. Back then, they suggested the greenhouse of carbon dioxide around the world might get too powerful, and rather than a nice layer to keep us warm we would end up with a thick layer trapping too much heat. And they were right. Carbon in our atmosphere is similar to fat on our bodies. We all need some fat to survive, just like the planet needs a basic amount of greenhouse gases to keep us warm. But too much fat is bad for you. Keep eating fatty foods, and eventually your metabolism and health change so much you're in a real crisis. Greenhouse gases are like fatty, sugary calories for the climate. They've been building up and clogging the atmosphere.

That's what Arrhenius was suggesting back when top hats and parasols were all the rage. But it took until the 1960s for computer models to show that just a 4-degree celsius increase in the global climate would have extraordinary and devastating effects on the planet's human passengers. Today we've already increased the temperature by over 1 degree. It doesn't sound like much, but that's quite a lot shaved off the table leg.

Heat and Ice

The main reason we know so much about our climate today is the Cold War. During those tense years (1947–91), both the American and Russian military became extremely interested in climate science and what affects it. Thick sea ice, for example, could stop a nuclear submarine from raising its periscope and contacting a command centre. So the military pumped a lot of money into understanding things like sea ice and tidal flows, desert conditions and air temperature. Today, the US Navy and NASA still generate some of the best data in the world on global warming, and the US Department of Defense named climate change a clear and current threat to global and national security.[1]

One of my favourite climate heroes from the cold war was a man called Charles Keeling (he died in 2005, after a world-changing career). As a young researcher he invented a machine that could test the level of carbon dioxide in the atmosphere more accurately than ever before. He had to travel to remote Big Sur, in California, and camp out, taking measurements in the clean air so that his very sensitive machine wouldn't be affected by any big industry nearby or by the millions of people breathing out carbon dioxide in a city. One man with a tent watching his measurement apparatus tick over, for weeks. His findings were spectacular. And worrying.

His gizmo worked so well, and taught us so much about global warming, that today two huge versions of it are quietly reading our carbon-dioxide levels from an unpolluted spot in Hawaii. Once an hour they pop out a number, and over time those numbers, when compared to others around the world, have told a very simple story: the carbon dioxide in our atmosphere is growing. And growing.

1. US Department of Defense, 'National Security Implications of Climate-Related Risks and a Changing Climate', *Climate Change Risks and Adaptation* (2015): 13–20.

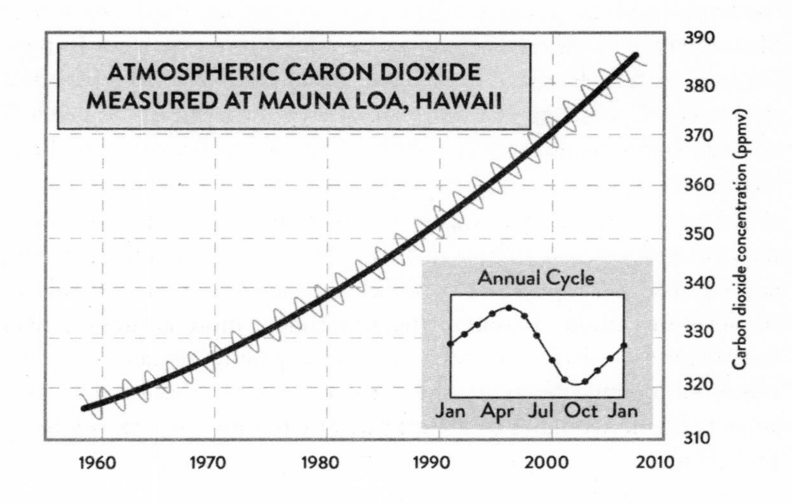

Figure 1. The Keeling Curve (source: Sémhur Narayanese and the NOAA)

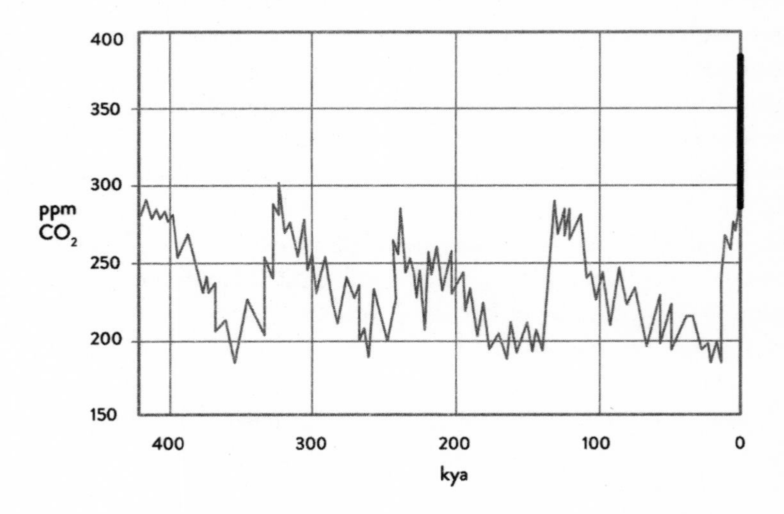

Figure 2. The Vostok ice core (kya = one thousand years). The light grey line is the measurement of carbon dioxide from the ice cores; the very thick black line on the far right is the Keeling Curve.

Keeling's machines have been running for only 50 years, which is a tiny window in terms of the planet's long climate history. But ice can take us further back. The French glaciologist Claude Lorius still remembers his own eureka moment. He was working in the Antarctic in incredibly cold and challenging conditions, trying to drill deep into the ice to study how it changed over time. One successful drill pulled up a long, intact core of ice that had been laid down thousands of years ago. His team broke out a bottle of cognac to celebrate, and cheekily added a few small chunks of that ancient ice to their drinks. As Dr Lorius raised his glass, he noticed the ice squeaking and cracking as it melted, and realised the noises were tiny bubbles of air being released. Standing there, it struck him: those bubbles of air were perfectly preserved samples of the earth's atmosphere from thousands of years ago.

His insight means that today we can test cores of ancient ice drilled out of glaciers and measure exactly how much carbon was in the air and what the temperature was going back nearly a million years. That means we know what the weather and the carbon-dioxide levels were back when sabre-toothed tigers and mammoths roamed the earth. From the warmth of a campsite in California to a frozen Antarctic base, the story is the same: when carbon levels are high, the planet warms. In past ages, carbon from huge volcanoes and other natural sources built up over centuries, and the climate was changed by it incredibly slowly – so slowly that the equally slow pace of evolution could keep up. But today, the spike in carbon is happening at super speed, much faster than our little planet has ever experienced before. With almost 350 parts per million of carbon dioxide in our atmosphere today, we're breathing air that is very different to that of our great-grandparents.

That carbon comes from us – from our fossil fuels. The term 'fossil fuels' basically means burnable carbon: petrol used in cars, coal, wood, natural gas and even the animal droppings burned in the poorest countries all release carbon dioxide. There are other gases that trap the heat too, such as methane (yep, farts), and with almost 2 billion grazing cattle that's a lot of fart. But the sheer amount of carbon dioxide in our atmosphere makes it the driving force behind climate change.

Trees absorb carbon as part of photosynthesis: that's the big biological bargain. We humans and all other animals breathe out carbon dioxide and breathe in oxygen. Trees and other plant life do the opposite, taking in carbon dioxide and pumping out oxygen. This was a fantastic balance until we started burning carbon as well as breathing it out and began cutting down a lot of trees. Now there simply isn't enough suitable plant life to suck up all the extra carbon, so it keeps building and building in the atmosphere, trapping too much heat.

People across the world are busily measuring all this carbon dioxide and its effects on our climate. From deep-sea temperature readings to upper-atmosphere weather balloons, we are building a detailed picture of the problem. And our supercomputers crunch through the numbers to tell us what's likely to happen. It's taken us this long to discover that while it might be hard to affect the weather, it's only too easy to change the climate. As my business partner Ed Gillespie puts it: 'Burning chemicals and cutting down all the big trees – what did we think would happen?'

That's how we got to this climate crossroads. We didn't mean to arrive here. No evil dictator rubbed his hands together and sneered: 'Mwah hah hah! Burn fossil fuels and cut down trees and we can create global climate change! My evil plan is almost complete!' People just got on with their lives. We built amazing things, grew our population, spread across the world, loved, lived and did what people do. We've always complained about the weather; we didn't realise we were changing it. Until now. We've already experienced huge dust clouds in China and terrible droughts in India; devastating storms in America and freezing weather and floods in Europe. In Australia it's started to get so hot they've had to introduce a new colour on their weather maps, while in the Pacific they've run out of names for superstorms and are just giving them numbers instead. Our emergency rescue teams, farming communities and even insurance companies are rewriting the rules to accommodate the changes that have already taken place.

Explaining climate change is daunting. It is a very big dragon for a new happy hero to slay. The sheer scale and history of it make me feel small, and it can sometimes be hard to remain positive when the threat seems so dark, big and nasty.

Until I remember that I already have the answer.

Changing the World

In 1939, with war against Germany looming, the British government designed a poster. They would be very surprised to know that it's now plastered across coffee cups, T-shirts and office walls. Because although the 'Keep Calm and Carry On' poster has become a contemporary favourite, in the end they decided not to use it during the war. Two and a half million copies of 'Keep Calm' were printed, but all bar a handful wound up being pulped. The poster that was actually used as war started, also featuring the crown of King George VI set against a bold red background, said: 'Your Courage, Your Cheerfulness, Your Resolution Will Bring Us Victory'. Not without controversy at the time (especially for using 'your' and 'us'), it is one of the most accurate war posters in history, because courage, cheerfulness and resolution are excellent descriptors of a happy and victorious hero!

During wartime, few argue against the importance of morale and the crucial necessity for the troops and the home front to believe in the inevitability of victory. As the great American president (and former military general) Dwight D. Eisenhower put it: 'Morale is the greatest single factor in successful wars.'

This isn't a mere platitude, because we human beings have a habit of adapting our behaviour to our expectations. If we assume we're going to lose, then we needn't bother trying. But assume we'll win and all our effort, courage and willingness to change will follow that assumption. A positive attitude counts. And this is the secret to facing down that large dragon of climate change, or indeed anything else, and unlocking a whole series of rewards as a result.

I'm going to argue that societies seem to have an uncanny knack for getting what they wish for. And that makes your happy-hero mindset much more important than you might think. Carl Jung was the first to popularise the fact that societies have their own 'collective unconscious' – all the themes, stories and assumptions that run through whole societies without being noticed or even planned. The Germans call it the '*Zeitgeist*', or 'the spirit of the time', and the scientist Richard Dawkins introduced the idea of 'memes', ideas that can travel through a population, self-replicating in the same way genes do.

But whether we call it the collective unconscious, zeitgeist or memes, it increasingly seems that the stories, attitudes and collective mindset of a population can have a direct impact on how that population will act. And this phenomenon is only heightened and hardened in our digital age, where we all participate in an endless big conversation about what our societies stand for. Appreciating this is vitally important if you want to save the world. With the wrong collective mindset at the crossroads it will become almost impossible to get people to take even the simplest and most obvious positive actions. With the right mindset, however, even the biggest changes will become easy to effect. If we want to solve climate change, then we need everyone on that smart pathway, feeling hopeful about the future. With the happy heroes up front, leading that change.

The Thomas Theorem

In 1928, the sociologist William Thomas and his wife, Dorothy, published a book on raising children. One sentence in that book became the foundation for a whole area of sociological science and is still the subject of experiments and doctoral theses today:

> *If men define situations as real, they are real in their consequences.*[2]

This means that if we believe something to be true, we'll work to make it so (consciously or subconsciously). Real-world examples of

2. William Isaac Thomas, 'The Methodology of Behavior Study', *The Child in America: Behavior Problems and Programs*, 93.15 (1928): 553–76 (web).

this axiom abound. One of my favourites dates back to 1973, when, during an oil shortage in the US, a rumour circulated that there would be a scarcity and rationing not just of petrol, but also toilet paper. People who heard the rumour crowded into stores to bulk-buy loo roll, and their bathrooms and garden sheds were turned over to stockpiling it. The demand for toilet paper soon became much greater than the supply, leading to local stores running out. The rumour wasn't true originally, but because enough people believed it, they made it so!

In the 1940s, another famous sociologist, Robert K. Merton, built on the Thomas Theorem and coined the better-known phrase 'self-fulfilling prophecy'. These ideas have become the bedrock of how scientists now look at social change: if we collectively believe something to be true, we'll start making it true. It's not magic, but Dr Merton himself pointed out that it is unique to us wonderful, complicated human beings: 'It is not found in the world of nature, untouched by human hands. Predictions of the return of Halley's comet do not influence its orbit.'

Both Thomas and Merton were worried about how self-fulfilling prophecies can lead to very negative outcomes, especially in terms of prejudice and war. Merton imagined two nations on the verge of conflict:

> It is believed that war between two nations is inevitable. Actuated by this conviction, representatives of the two nations become progressively alienated, apprehensively countering each 'offensive' move of the other with a 'defensive' move of their own. Stockpiles of armaments, raw materials, and armed men grow larger and eventually the anticipation of war helps create the actuality.[3]

Self-fulfilling prophecies have been discovered lurking within small family groups and all the way up to entire nations. Our collective expectations can make (or break) economies because of panics or confidence bubbles. Billionaire investor George Soros has written books

3. Robert K. Merton, 'The Self-Fulfilling Prophecy', *The Antioch Review*, 8.2 (1948): 193–210.

about how positive and negative collective mindsets affect financial markets, and regards his insights into this phenomenon during the recession as a major factor in his success. Soros calls his philosophy 'reflexivity' and says that Thomas's and Merton's work convinced him that financial markets aren't stable machines, but rather collections of human beings susceptible to herd-like behaviour: 'My conceptual framework enabled me both to anticipate the crisis and to deal with it when it finally struck. It has also enabled me to explain and predict events better than most others.'[4]

So why does this all matter so much?

Because collectively we believe we are either going up or down the crisis curve. And depending on what we expect, the Thomas Theorem dictates that we'll somehow manage to make it true. Believe we're all doomed, and then there's no point acting to avoid disaster, thereby actually guaranteeing it. But believe the future can be awesome, then by preparing for that, you'll radically increase our chances of getting there.

The same is true for any belief about climate change. Either we the public believe we can solve it or we don't. And this belief is more important than any regulation or technology could ever be.

Imagine a venture capitalist with money to invest in a technology. That person must decide to spend their money on either a new solar panel or new fracking equipment for oil extraction. To help in their choice they'll likely review the numbers, look at the business plans and check the projections for getting a big return on their money. But they will also base their decision on their subconscious expectations of what the future will be like. Will more people want solar panels or oil? This is how our collective attitude, expectations and action can influence huge investment and policy decisions about our future – sometimes even if the person making those decisions isn't aware of it.

4. George Soros, 'Fallibility, Reflexivity, and the Human Uncertainty Principle', *Journal of Economic Methodology*, 20.4 (2013): 309–29.

Changing the Tide

Today we happy heroes need to become venture *optimists*. Because if we believe that the future is going to be clean, green, fair and wonderful, then our decisions – conscious and subconscious – will help make that come true. We need to passionately believe that our children's lives can be better than ours, more safe, fulfilling and happy. In fact, we need to believe that is possible during our own lives. I call this 'self-fulfilling *positivity*', and it's a core part of the happy-hero formula. Not only will your positive, optimistic mindset reward you personally, but because of the Thomas Theorem, your attitude will play a huge part in making everyone's future beautiful.

But just like there is no simple switch for feeling positive about yourself, nor is there a 'belief in the future' switch. So, how can happy heroes make sure that whole societies have the right attitude for heading up the curve?

Convince Yourself

In this chapter we've seen how important collective optimism and self-fulfilling positivity are. But what do we have to be optimistic about? Later, I'm going to take you on a worldwide tour of exactly what is going to change for the better. For this formula to work you need to truly believe we can do this, that we *can* make the world a better place for ourselves and our children. It might take a lot of hard work, but in Chapter 4 (and at thehappyhero.org) you'll find proof that we can do it.

Convince Others

We are all surrounded by pessimism and dystopia, and understandably so. Bad things happen. In fact, terrible and terrifying things happen, and the internet gives us intimate, unending and overwhelming access to those bad things. That's the tide we're facing, and some people will think we are naïve or uninformed if we stay optimistic. But we must share good and positive examples and news stories with our friends, families, neighbours and online communities. In the next chapter, we'll talk about how hope can sometimes threaten people who are scared and angry. But there are ways to overcome that – even if you need to overcome it in yourself first.

Do Something

Remember the power of the feedback loop in the happy-hero formula (see Chapter 1)? The very best way to feel hopeful is to do something positive. The Thomas Theorem isn't just about our underlying attitudes, it's about how these directly affect our actions. In Chapter 4, 'Learning Heroism', you're going to discover your own tailor-made 'Happy Hero Action Plan', with small and large ways to make a better world and a better you. And every time you do one thing on that list you'll find that your hope, positivity and optimism shoot up.

By now you should be convinced that optimism and positivity are important both for your own well-being and also for societies as a whole when facing problems. But even if you find the evidence for the power of hope compelling, you might still be struggling to really feel it yourself.

In the next chapter we'll meet the guards inside your brain who are blocking your journey to happy heroism. They might be familiar when you meet them, or they might take you completely by surprise. Either way, they are blocking your entry to the world you want, so it's time to get you past them and on to your wonderful life.

*

The Story of a Happy Hero

'Are you coming?' Jane's friend Aisha asked over her shoulder as she walked past her desk.

'Huh? Coming to what?' Jane answered, looking up and trying to refocus her eyes after staring at her screen for too long.

'There's a talk in the cafeteria this afternoon. With free cake, apparently.' Aisha stopped and smiled as she explained. 'Something about corporate responsibility and, well, all I remember is the cake bit, to be honest. Come with me!'

Jane stretched back in her chair for a moment and then got up. 'I do fancy a break. Although just to be clear, this has nothing to do with the cake.'

Aisha laughed and led the way out. The cafeteria was quite full when they arrived and all the seats had been moved to face a cleared space. They sat down towards the back and were surprised when the CEO herself walked in to open the meeting.

'Thank you all for joining me here today,' the CEO said. 'As you know, we've always prided ourselves on being a responsible business. And today I'm here to talk about some big changes we want to make. Specifically, I want us to discuss how, as a business, we should respond to the challenge of climate change.'

Jane almost jumped out of her chair.

The mysterious 'Godmother' in her online group had suggested that her family make a plan to start taking action. Although she'd been enthusiastic initially, she was just too busy the next day to get started on it, and the day after. Ben seemed to have recovered from the scare he'd had at school about climate change, and her workload had piled up. She had almost forgotten about the whole thing. But she still hadn't logged back onto the site, in case the Godmother asked her if she'd done anything yet. But now the issue had come up again. And to think she'd come mainly for the cake.

'I don't believe that climate change is only a risk for our company, but also that solving this issue is the greatest entrepreneurial opportunity of our lifetime. In fact, I've found in my own life that cutting carbon has true benefits. For the past month I've been cycling to our offices rather than using my company car. And I shall be enjoying a slice of cake in a moment, knowing that I've earned it.' Everyone in the room laughed with polite but genuine mirth at the idea of their rather formal CEO on a bicycle.

'Now,' she went on, 'does anyone have any great new ideas for how we can make a difference?' Down towards the front a few hands shot up. It turned out people had a lot of ideas, from improving recycling to changing how products were trucked around the country.

Jane turned with astonishment when Aisha's hand slowly went up. The CEO pointed to her, and Aisha spoke tentatively. 'Umm, what about at home and things like that? Is there a way the company could help us to do our own bit?' All eyes were turned her way, and most people looked a little perplexed.

The CEO's face was blank as she probed Aisha. 'I'm not sure I understand that question. Aren't we already discussing ways the company can take action?'

Jane could see a deep red flush starting to move up Aisha's neck as her friend struggled to explain. 'What I meant… Well, we all try to do things, I guess. You know, at home. But maybe the company could… I mean, all of us trying… umm…' Aisha's voice was getting quieter as her cheeks got pinker.

'You could help us to buy a bicycle,' Jane suddenly said loudly. 'The company could loan us employees money to buy bikes and helmets. So then we can all cycle into work, just like you!' Jane hadn't planned to speak, but as her friend struggled, the idea had just popped into her head and out of her mouth at the same time.

The CEO was silent for a moment. Then she clapped her hands together and smiled. 'Excellent idea! We could establish a company-wide cycle scheme. I even believe the government offers support for that sort of thing. I know cycling has done wonders for me. Right, any more ideas like that?'

The meeting went on, and Aisha turned to Jane with the grateful look of someone who had just been saved from certain death.

Jane was feeling something a bit different. A kind of warm pride was building in her, not only because she'd helped her friend, but because her idea really was a good one. Even though she'd just thought of it, a whole list of reasons why it should happen started to fill her mind: the stressful drive in; rows and rows of cars in the company car park and the struggle to find a spot; never having time to exercise. But biking would solve all that at once.

She couldn't stop thinking about it all day and wondering if the CEO would actually do anything about the idea. And she laughed out loud to herself on her drive home when she remembered she hadn't even had any cake.

3

How much easier it is to be critical than to be correct.

—Benjamin Disraeli

Most of this book gives directions for the road up the curve to success. In the coming chapters, you're going to learn how to apply the mindset that makes a difference and then enjoy the fantastic personal rewards that will bring. You'll discover an entire new way of living better, and you'll meet the people who are making that happen. Towards the end of the book there are even some big surprises about our future and your role in it.

But before you enter this new world there are two terrifying guards you must first pass. They aren't the only obstacles you'll face, but they are the ones that prevent most people from making their happy-hero journey. They are the dangerous mindsets and compelling excuses for inaction you need to recognise as you work your way through. So, before we get to the 'how to', let's take a look at the 'how *not* to' of positive change.

Bad Mindsets

You'll have already noticed that 'hope' and 'optimism' aren't terms we usually hear in relation to the future. Instead, throughout our media, in online debates and even in our families we often avoid conversation about the future entirely. And if big issues like climate change are mentioned, it's usually as part of a political argument or because of some new bad news.

But what we should be doing is planning our bright future and getting our kids excited about tomorrow. That's the happy-hero mindset. Too often we don't let ourselves happily plot a positive picture of our lives, and that's because of two mindsets that block the conversation, or even stop us thinking positively at all. Again, I'm going to use climate change as our dragon and cast these two mindsets as its evil henchmen. But remember that these insights can be used for any challenge on the way to greatness, be it large ones in our societies or small ones in our lives.

I want you to imagine two giant orc-like guardians blocking your path. They might not be very smart, but they are very powerful, and you're going to have to either fight or trick your way around them before you can go any further.

- **The Monster of Denial.** The denial monsters bellow at you that nothing is true, or that threats are completely overblown. They believe in ominous conspiracies and cabals plotting against them. While they claim to be realists, they are often just scared of progress. When it comes to climate change, the monster of denial is backed by huge vested interests (such as the coal and oil industries) trying to protect the 'normal' point we've already passed in the crisis curve. And these monsters just don't like environmentalists much. Science won't sway them (other heroes have tried before), and their superpower is that attacking them just makes them stronger. However, there is a way past them, and it might not be the one you expect.
- **The Monster of Doom.** Doom monsters are masters of fear and guilt. They paint a picture of the worst possible outcomes, and tell you it's all your fault. They are called 'worthy', the 'anti-everything' or the 'hippie hair-shirt' brigade. They are Chicken Little convincing you the sky is going to fall. They flagellate you for being bad and destined for a bad end. Their superpower is a guilt so total it will send you into apathy and avoidance. They will suck your energy away and convince you that the only way out of the curve is downwards. They are harder to defeat than the Monster of Denial, and might already be sneaking around in your mind. But they also have their weak spots, and can even be cured.

These two guards are the king and queen of Negativity Land. And they hate each other passionately. Denialists and doomists call each other 'trolls', 'terrorists', 'loons' and 'psychos' online, and they take up most of the comments sections in any online post about climate change (they seem to have a surprising amount of time on their hands). Most of us would probably agree with the mud they sling at each other, even if we can't remember which insult applies to which group.

Many normal people who deny or are a bit doomy have just been tricked into these two downer mindsets. Once you kick the door open a little and allow some light into the darkness, then most people are smart enough to step through.

Assuming they can get around these two guys…

Dealing with Denial

The real puzzle of climate change has always been why so many people so vehemently believe it's not happening. Of course, climate change isn't the only thing people deny. Conspiracy theories thrive when cultures face a crisis curve, and they are nothing more than an overly complicated way to deny reality.

Wishful thinking that climate change isn't that bad is a maladaptation we'll deal with later on, but denial has a harder edge. I know because I sometimes get tweets, emails and even phone calls from denialists, and I study them carefully. The hatred and accusations are hurtful, but also weirdly fascinating. The writers or callers are almost always anonymous, and they assume that climate change is part of a huge, well-coordinated and complex global conspiracy – be it left-wing or right-wing. They make me a little wistful about how cool a real conspiracy would be, with assignations, code words and deals made in darkened rooms. But no one has invited me to join a secret cabal yet.

Feeling powerless in the face of something (or someone) big is the root cause of denial. The doom monsters don't help much either, by reinforcing the message that climate change is huge and all-powerful. Unintentionally, the climate-doom message feeds powerlessness, which then feeds denial.

A recent study tested all this.[1] Researchers split people into two groups. One was told to write about times when they were totally in control, and the other was told to write about a time when they felt powerless. Those in the first group experienced a boost in their own sense of power, while the others were primed to feel helpless. The researchers then tested the two groups' belief in conspiracy theories and their denial of evidence. Those who had been reminded of a time when they were in control were less likely to be sucked into the conspiracy/denial mindset, whereas the others became more open to it.

It's as if our own sense of power inoculates us against being drawn into conspiracy theories and denial, but a sense of helplessness leaves us vulnerable to 'post-truth' messages and manipulation.

Taking this further, when people are reminded of their own personal successes and challenges they have overcome, they are less likely to deny larger or global problems. Think about that for a moment. All those arguments, all that anger, all those big problems people have with accepting climate change can start to disappear when they are reminded of how powerful and successful they are. Try it. Think right now about a time when you made a difference to your kids, helped someone else, argued your case or even kept a promise – a time when you were in control. And keep remembering that whenever the monster of denial creeps up on you. Most of us get a bit 'denially' (about many things) when we feel small and weak. The strong don't deny; they decide.

The instigators of denialist movements have more serious psychological problems than most of those who just listen or feel a bit denially. Looking at a range of denialist movements, social psychologist Dr Seth C. Kalichman worryingly concluded that their leaders 'display all the features of paranoid personality disorder', including anger and intolerance of criticism. Kalichman, who is from the University of Connecticut, concludes that for the worst conspiracy theorists, 'ultimately, their denialism is a mental-health problem. That is why these movements all have the same features.'[2]

1. Jan-Willem Van Prooijen and Michele Acker, 'The Influence of Control on Belief in Conspiracy Theories: Conceptual and Applied Extensions', *Applied Cognitive Psychology*, 29.5 (2015): 753–61.

2. 'Living in Denial', *New Scientist* Special Report, May 2010.

Most of us feel tempted by denial sometimes, but we don't start movements or organisations dedicated to it. For most of us, the tendency towards denial is a psychological refuge against fear. If we are offered payback from action and the vision of a great future instead, the need for that refuge dissolves.

The Root of Denial

Denial springs from four main sources, three of which are totally natural, but one of which is damned nasty:

- **Fear.** Big problems like climate change are just too scary to deal with. People simply don't want it to be real because they feel too small. This is the most common cause of denial, and it is made much worse when people already feel a low sense of control or self-esteem.
- **Confusion.** Big problems can feel too complicated, global and 'sciencey'. It can't be happening because 'If I don't understand it, then no one else can.' Another version of this is pure disbelief that things like climate change could ever go so wrong.
- **Reactance.** This is a fancy name for what happens when people don't like environmentalists. Personal dislike of 'hippie liberal types' leads to mistrust of climate data, and the personality clashes make people double down on their denial. Conspiracy theories born here often include a lot of bile and anger. The green types themselves don't help when they fuel this reactance by antagonising people.

Feeling afraid of big issues like climate change, getting confused and being annoyed at shrill environmentalists are all totally natural reactions at this point in the crisis curve. But with a slight change of mindset and a promise of payback from action, people can overcome them. The fourth source of denial is a lot harder to address because it's not natural at all:

- **Money.** Unfortunately, many denialist movements start as cynical efforts by corporations or 'vested interests' to cast doubt on science that threatens their bottom line. It might be easier to accept if they at least tried to cover up their efforts. Big tobacco[3] started it in the 1970s, bankrolling think tanks and bogus grass-roots movements and recruiting scientists who were willing to produce data to show that smoking wasn't dangerous. One such think tank was The Advancement of Sound Science Coalition (TASSC), set up in 1993 by tobacco company Philip Morris. TASSC published data for years arguing that there was no scientific basis for claims of any relationship between smoking and cancer. And after getting funds from Exxon, it then cast doubt on climate science. These arch-manipulators accuse rather geeky and socially inept scientists of trying to manipulate the public on climate change. One of my favourite tweets ever about the irony of the situation goes: 'Plot idea: 97% of the world's scientists contrive an environmental crisis, but are exposed by a plucky band of billionaires and oil companies!' This would be a good point at which to feel a smidgeon of righteous anger, but then get over it. This sort of thing is enough to drive anyone into conspiracy-theory land. But don't go there; it will just make you feel small. Just get on with being a happy hero instead.

Defeating the Monster of Denial

Above all else, don't get angry with actual people (although being angry with those organisations that manipulate people is fine). The crossroads of the crisis curve is a pretty scary place, and denial is only to be expected. But getting all shouty or being 'holier than thou' will just make it all worse. Accept that you might have felt denial yourself – in fact, you might still be feeling it a bit. From climate change to problems with our own health, relationships or lives, denial is a natural part of the journey to heroism and is often the first step towards positive change.

Here are a few strategies for overcoming this monster:

1. **Climate change is the enemy, not the person who denies it.** Remember that you hate climate change and that it's normal to be scared of it. So there's no point hating

3. 'Defending Hot Air: TASSC Takes on Global Warming', *PR Watch*, 4.3 (1997): 12.

people for a normal reaction. Focus instead on how excited you are about a future without it. That payback from action can help inoculate against denial.

2. **Leave the hard science to the scientists.** Investigate the proofs of climate science as much as you need to (and that might be a lot), but don't try to memorise every point. There are hundreds of clear, detailed, technical or simple explanations of the science. If someone is in denial, then giving them a science lesson isn't going to help. Find out why they are in denial, and point them to independent and robust sources only in the unlikely case that a lack of information is their real problem.

3. **Remember that a desire for denial is a totally natural human response to threat.** Take care not to become 'pro-climate change'. Occasionally, people get so passionate when talking about the problem they sound like they are fans of it!

4. **Be nice, not nasty, to others in denial.** Remember that denial is a 'psychological reactance'. Therapists treat people with kindness and compassion when they are in denial, because when people feel good about themselves and safe they are more open to considering new ideas. Smile. Ask people questions about themselves, empathise and strengthen them to the point where they can take on anything – including the crisis curve.

5. **Be funny if you want.** Denial may be about fear and anger, but cracking a few jokes diffuses tension and invites people in. Personally, I favour bad British humour. The fact that very important government leaders have to discuss how cows farting is causing climate change should get you started. Especially if they had beans for lunch.

I've successfully managed my own tendency towards denial, and helped others, with these strategies. Kindness and understanding go a long way to getting past this monster, because really it's just scared. If you get a chance, give it a hug.

Then turn your attention to the other monster, but be prepared: a hug is unlikely to help in this case.

Dealing with Doom

A few years ago I invented a way to diagnose the 'doom monster' mindset. It's called the Climate Fairy Test.

I was in the US making a speech to nearly 200 hard-core, deeply green environmentalists. I asked them to imagine that I was a supernatural being called the Climate Fairy who could scrub all the excess carbon dioxide out of our atmosphere. With just one wave of my sparkly magic wand I could make sure we never ever went beyond 2 degrees of global warming. But – and it's a pretty big but – I would be interfering with the laws of physics, not with psychology, so everyone in the world could continue being as selfish, status-driven and consumption-obsessed as they are now. Cars and houses would get bigger, planes would fly all over the place – but magically, there would be no climate change. No climate change at all, and no one would have to feel guilty, change their behaviour or admit environmentalists had been right all along. The catch for the Climate Fairy is that, as with all fairies, her magic only comes from wishes. How many in the audience would wish for me to wave my wand? I asked.

Of the 200 people in the room, only two raised their hands.

I asked the rest of the audience why they wouldn't wish for me to save the world. The answers were not well articulated, but they were quite consistent. These people were angry. Many of them had been angry for a long time: angry at consumption culture, angry at big business, angry at 'keeping up with the Joneses', angry at reality TV, at McDonald's-isation, at celebrity magazines… These people were angry and disappointed with their fellow human beings; they wanted them to change and become 'better people'.

I wouldn't want the fairy to wave her wand either, not unless it was totally necessary. But that's because I want the big rewards from solving climate change. I want more excitement, more discovery and a better life. I believe we will change because we want to. There is no magic wand, but if we wish and work very hard, we can all enjoy a better life, and solve climate change in the process.

And we know that hope is more likely to save us than fear. In 2006, the research group ESRC reviewed 129 different studies of how people change their behaviour for the better, and they found that the least effective motivator was fear or regret. Doom simply doesn't work.

Nor does trying to make people 'better' and less interested in celebrities or shopping. And I don't care if you're obsessed with celebrity magazines – I am too. I don't care if you love foreign holidays – they are brilliant and I know I look much better with a tan. There is absolutely nothing wrong with wanting all the things that are bad for the environment. It's what normal people across the world want. The trick is to want even better things. As we'll see in Chapter 7, 'A Good Life', we can all be climate fairies and enjoy ourselves in the process.

That mindset is the antidote to doom. But some doomists don't so much fight against climate change as wag their finger and proclaim we all deserve it. There are those who think the world would be 'better off without humans', those who want to punish sinful humanity for being disconnected from nature, for being selfish and for being, well, human. Not all environmentalists are like this; some are just battle-weary. They have fought against climate change, without much support, for too long. They deserve our backing and thanks for fighting alone. It's mostly possible to reignite their fire, especially with a bit of positivity.

The Root of Doom

The worst doom monsters are more akin to 'the-end-is-nigh', Bible-thumping, burn-in-hell missionaries. They want you to repent. They want you to admit your sins. They want you to change your values to be more like them. They are dangerous to have hanging around at the crossroads of a crisis curve because they give very bad advice on which road to take. If you're not careful, they'll convince you that you built the crisis curve and so you deserve to walk down the road to disaster.

These apocalypse junkies come from the same point of fear as the denialists. For them, being right is more important than doing right. Some people deny climate change because they don't like doomy environmentalists, and some environmentalists spread doom because they don't like people.

'The End of the Universe is very popular,' said Zaphod in Douglas Adams's wonderful book *The Restaurant at the End of the Universe*. 'People like to dress up for it… gives it a sense of occasion.' This is from the chapter in the book where diners enjoy watching the obliteration of life, the universe and everything, while tucking into a nice steak. That's what the doomists are like, except you don't get the steak.

Some of them believe that most of us are going to be washed away by climate change, but a few survivors will then live in harmony with nature in an *Avatar*-type state. There are even festivals dedicated to doom, with sessions called 'How will we choose to live out the last years of the Holocene and mark its passing?' They sit around talking about biodiversity collapse and financial crisis, with a dollop of climate meltdown thrown in (all with a song, poem or workshop moodily celebrating it).

Defeating the Monster of Doom

We humans quite like an apocalypse story. Disaster movies and dystopic novels are very popular. We're drawn to them.

But climate change isn't a story. And it is truly scary, although it constantly surprises me how many people seem to enjoy the worry rather than rolling up their sleeves to do something about it. Nothing in this book should ever be used to suggest that climate change is anything other than the greatest threat we've ever faced on this planet, not least because it's not just a 'potential' threat, like nuclear war, but an enormous problem that is already playing out. The 'bombs' are already in the air.

But even so, there is zero benefit in giving up. Believing 'we're all doomed', as we know from the Thomas Theorem (see Chapter 2), would pretty much guarantee that we will be. So instead I'm going to pit my little light of hope against the giant darkness of my fear, like David against Goliath. And we all know how that turned out.

And I'm also going to remember that, in all the most popular apocalypse stories, there are always heroes fighting to turn back the disaster. And they seem to have a lot more fun than the extras in the background who are meekly accepting their fate. It also helps that I know how many brilliant, hard-working and creative happy heroes I have working alongside me in this, with more and more of you joining every day.

So how do you deal with the doom monsters out there or in your own head? Here are some strategies:

1. **Don't make light of climate change.** One danger of the doom mindset is that you can sound like a denialist when you're trying to cheer the monster up! Be clear that, while you know it's bad, you're not just going to surrender to it. Not least because the rewards of solving climate change are so rich.
2. **Ask the doom monsters themselves for a solution.** This also works when you're feeling doomy yourself. Challenges to think creatively about solutions can help you snap out of the doom mindset. Just thinking about a plan can make it feel achievable.
3. **Think of our previous great crises.** From war to disease, previous generations have stood in the darkness or at their own crossroads, and many people then also assumed the worst. Global horrors like the slave trade were just as deeply embedded in society, the economic system and daily life as fossil fuels are today. Many couldn't even imagine a time without that horrendous trade, and others even fought to keep it. Yet after slavery was outlawed, life without it felt just as normal as life with it. Enormous and transformational changes to the system do happen, often at speed, if enough people desire it.
4. **Find their real problem.** For some people climate change is just a symptom of other things they find upsetting, from rampant consumerism to human destruction of nature. The disconnect many feel between their own values and the wider values in society can lead to a 'we deserve it' reaction to climate change. Feeling upset at the disconnect is justified: it's very hard when values collide. Thinking that 'we deserve it' isn't, because no one deserves the kind of punishment climate change could dish out. Although it might be satisfying to read stories in which punishment rains down on the sinful, the reality isn't

satisfying, and it's also rarely fair. But the rewards of doing good will be!

5. **Remind yourself that doom is more likely to inspire apathy than action.** Many doomists have just spent too long arguing with denialists, and doom has become a refuge. But at heart, almost every doom monster is just a happy hero who has been tricked off the right path. By focusing on action and being excited about the future, most doomists will choose to join the community of happy heroes instead.

Above all else, when doom rears its head, remember: you *are* strong enough, you *are* smart enough, and together we can boost ourselves out of the crisis curve and take a peek at the wonders waiting down the road. We're even going to drag all the denial and doom monsters over with us, because that's just the type of hero we are.

As the bumbling human hero Arthur Dent asks in *The Restaurant at the End of the Universe*, as his friends skip out on their bill:

> 'But what about the End of the Universe? We'll miss the big moment.'
>
> 'I've seen it. It's rubbish,' said Zaphod. [...] 'Come on, let's get zappy.'

*

The Story of a Happy Hero

The car wheels screeched to a stop.

'What the hell are you doing?' Jane heard as a car door was flung open. She carefully wobbled her bike to a stop. 'I could have killed you!' Her dad was standing looking at her, flabbergasted, fighting the anger on his face. She had just been about to try cycling on the road for the first time when her father's car had pulled sharply into the drive.

'Grandad!' Ben shouted gleefully as he stepped around his mum and the bike. 'I'm teaching Mum to ride a bike!'

'What on earth for?' Jane's dad replied, turning sharply from Ben to her. 'What's wrong with your car?'

'Look, Dad, it's OK, nothing's wrong,' she said, having caught her breath after the shock of nearly being hit. 'My car's fine,' she assured him. 'I just wanted a change, that's all. And anyway, this is more fun!'

Her dad still looked exasperated. 'Another get-fit plan, is it? Don't know why you couldn't just go for a walk or something rather than spending all this money on a bike you can't even ride! I could have hit you just then. You've got to be more careful.'

'Don't worry, Grandad.' Ben came up and laid a hand on his mum's shiny new handlebars. 'I'm teaching her. I know the cycling code. And you were driving really fast anyway.'

With only a 'harrumph' for a reply and a tousle of his grandson's hair, Jane's father walked inside the house, while she carefully locked her new bike against the garden fence. She couldn't help a little smile as she looked at it leaning there, glinting in the sun. The CEO had started the cycle scheme within a week of her question at the meeting in the cafeteria, and Jane had been one of the first to sign up.

Her dad was just scooping a tea bag out of a freshly brewed cup as she came in. 'Don't put that in the bin, Dad,' she said quickly. 'Pop it in that green box on the counter, for the compost.' Her father turned around slowly, with his tea bag still sitting on the spoon and releasing little brown droplets onto his shoe. 'What's going on here?

Bikes… compost? I was only here a week ago and there was none of this.'

Jane stepped forward and grabbed her new compost caddy off the counter, holding it open below the dripping tea bag. With a slightly uncomfortable look her dad let the bag fall in. 'We're just making a few changes, Dad. As a family. Ben's in charge. He's been learning about environmental things at school. So we've made a plan to be a bit greener together. He's loving it! And I have to say, Dad, learning to cycle is the most fun I've had in years.'

'So it's a school project, then?' her father replied. 'Ben's doing it in class?'

'No, Dad. We decided to do it as a family,' Jane answered. She took a deep breath as she went on. 'We're going to cut our carbon footprint and try to be a bit healthier at the same time. Less driving, saving energy and doing our bit to stop climate change.'

Her dad suddenly looked angry again. 'I don't know what Ben's been hearing in class, but you should know better. All that climate stuff is just poppycock. Dreamed up by a bunch of London loonies to get their own way.' His face started to flush. 'Saving energy is all right, I suppose. I'm always telling you you need to turn off the lights in here. But climate change is a con. You can't go changing everything because of that.'

She'd been expecting this, but she wished Ben wasn't hearing it. Making a plan together to be a bit greener had really cheered him up; she hadn't realised that he had still been quietly worried about climate change. And she had to admit she was enjoying it too.

'Well, Dad' – she decided to answer diplomatically – 'why don't you help us with the saving energy bit, then? You've done wonders with your place. And whether it's to save money or carbon, you're great at it.' Her dad looked a bit mollified at the compliment, as she went on quickly: 'Maybe you and Ben could find some ways to stop this ticking over so fast.' She walked over to the cupboard and picked up their new wireless energy meter. As she handed it over she noticed the numbers showing electricity usage were clocking up. Her dad's face smoothed from anger lines into the calm expression he got when tinkering with gadgets in his tool shed. Ben stood alongside him on tiptoe to see.

Suddenly, Jane felt a flash of inspiration. 'Tell you what, Ben. If you and your grandad can figure out ways to save some energy around here, then I'll give you the money you've saved off our bill as this week's pocket money.'

Ben smiled gleefully, grabbed his grandfather's hand and said, 'C'mon, Grandad, let's save some energy. I want a new Pokémon deck.'

4

Learning Heroism

Whether you think you can, or think you can't, you are right.

—Henry Ford

At this point in the book I feel bit like a combination of Morpheus from *The Matrix*, the good witch Glinda from Oz and Yoda from *Star Wars*. And I'm calling upon this strange but powerful mix of teachers because I have some magical lessons for you.

In this chapter you are going learn five superhero skills. These will help you to:

- Know who you are and what heroic actions suit you;
- how to believe in and trust yourself…
- … while having fun making a difference…
- … working together in a team to which we all belong…
- … and holding onto hope and positivity every day.

Most importantly, throughout every lesson, we're going to change your mind, because, as that great teacher of humanity Shakespeare wrote: 'All things be ready, if our minds be so.'

Hope Swims

I remember vividly the first time I heard about Margaret Crotty. It was 1996 and I was a fresh-faced graduate, backpacking across the US. I ended up in a scruffy train station near Chicago, with barely a cent in my pocket and hours till my train was due. To pass the time I was reading through back copies of magazines that were lying around the station. And one story I read that night has stayed with me ever since.

Earlier that same year, an overloaded ferry sank in an unexpected storm off the coast of Sumatra, in Indonesia, killing 340 people. Among the handful of survivors was an American girl the same age I was that summer – just 23. After graduating from Princeton University, she had been working in Indonesia for Save the Children, travelling from village to village holding empowerment workshops for women.

Margaret had boarded the doomed ferry to make a two-hour trip to Weh Island. She said:

> It was the weekend before Ramadan, a month-long holiday, so the ferry was overcrowded. It left three hours late, after dark, and it didn't occur to me that it might be unsafe. An hour and twenty minutes after we took off, the boat slowed down. It almost came to a stop and tilted to the side. People ran to one side to compensate, but the boat tilted again. I knew something was wrong.

Margaret had hit the crisis curve – the whole ferry had. With more than 400 people on board the 555-ton *Gurita*, there weren't enough life jackets for everyone.

> People were panicking. They started jumping over the side into the water. I went to the life-jacket cabinet. I started to give out life jackets. I knew I had to do it because no one else was.

Margaret didn't keep a life jacket for herself. Having qualified as a lifeguard years before, she knew she was a strong swimmer.

> The boat was going down. There was this disbelief. Then I fell into the cabinet when the boat jolted. I was stuck inside this cabinet, but I was calm. I was thinking, 'This is what it is like to die.' It was dark. The boat was underwater, and I was inhaling water. I thought, 'I can't believe I'm dying. '

I find it hard to imagine the crossroads Margaret faced: the fear, the darkness, the water rising and the screams, the disorientation and the despair. She could have gone down, quite literally, with the ship.

> I then had this burst of thinking about my family. I thought, 'I can't let this happen.' I was trapped in the cabinet on the boat, underwater. I can't remember how I got out of the cabinet. The boat was fully under water, but then I was free. I swam up to the surface. There were people all around. I thought it was over, that I had a brush with death and now I was fine.

For the purposes of this book, we could stop here. Margaret hit her crossroads, found hope and swam ashore. Neat and inspirational. But the real inspiration is not her 20-minute fight or flight out of the boat, but the 16-hour ordeal that followed, testing that young woman's courage and ingenuity to the limit:

> There was a lifeboat with fifty or sixty people. I was treading water near it with some other people. One guy said there were sharks swimming beneath us. The Indonesians were praying. Then the life raft popped and deflated. People were holding on to me. My ankle was swollen. I had a deep cut, so I took my shirt to use as a bandage. I took off my pants, I learned this in lifeguard school. You tie them at the ankle, blow it up, and use it as a flotation device. I had a ball of air. It was 8:30 at night, dark. I was watching people panic and die so I was being rational. I had to help the other people get safe because they were panicking. I had to remain calm. I gave away my float.

For the next day, Margaret swam, without the float she'd given away. She was swept out of sight of anyone else. She swam with a bleeding wound in salt water. She swam when the sun came up and burned her exposed skin. With a parched mouth, stiffening limbs, bleeding, blistered and burned, still she swam.

She finally climbed onto a viciously sharp coral atoll and clung onto it for hours until, finally, she was rescued by fishermen.

Perhaps it's no surprise that Margaret's story has stuck with me for over 15 years. I've told it to friends, thought about it when facing my own challenges and learned from it what it takes to survive.

Hope isn't weak. Hope swims.

Academic research, books and personal stories of survival are almost unanimous on what it takes to survive a crisis. In first-hand accounts, the story is the same again and again: decide to die and you die; decide to survive – even in the face of laughably bad odds – and you could live. This is what Dr Dennis Charney, the dean of Mount Sinai School of Medicine, found when he interviewed 750 Vietnam War veterans who were held alongside others as prisoners of war for between six and eight years each. All were tortured and kept in solitary confinement, but these 750 men within the wider group were remarkably resilient. Unlike many fellow veterans, none of them developed depression or post-traumatic stress disorder after their release, despite what they had endured. What was their secret? After extensive interviews and tests, Dr Charney found that what set them apart was simple: optimism and altruism. They hoped, and they helped others.

This isn't a book about survival. At least I hope that's not what you're facing. But these stories prove that happy heroism isn't a shallow thing. Although most of your rewards will be smaller than surviving a disaster, they will still be powerful. This formula can change you, very deeply.

Everyday Extraordinary

Very few of us are born extraordinary. Most of us just work our way through life, being decent people, putting food on the table and having some fun. My cousin Stephanie is currently 'fostering' five rescue dogs from the local animal shelter to avoid them being put down. That's a lot of dogs in a house with four kids and a husband who's often away for long deployments in the US military. My youngest sister, Francesca, set up a support group for adults with mental-health diagnoses, and my other sister, Sian, decided she couldn't live with the environmental impact of using disposable nappies for her daughter, so now washes reuseable ones. All three will be horribly embarrassed that I'm using them as examples of happy heroism because, to them, what they are doing doesn't feel that momentous. In fact, most of the time they feel like they aren't making enough of a difference. But to me they are truly happy heroes because each has found ways (more than I could list here) of making the world a slightly better place.

We all have our moments of doubt or worry – and, sometimes, acute embarrassment. I once made an hour-long speech to a packed room of very smart folk at Harvard University, which was followed by intense questioning from PhD students and masters of the universe (a few MIT people had popped over too). Tough crowd, tough questions, and it was all being streamed live online. Afterwards, my host complimented me on how confident and energetic I'd been. I smiled wanly and thanked her, and didn't mention that I'd thrown up just before going on. I also kept it secret for years that I had almost forgotten my name during the introductions. Thankfully, it was up on the PowerPoint slide behind me. All those people had been impressed by my speech, but hadn't realised I'd been so intimidated that I had had to use a slide to remember my own name.

Once someone becomes a happy hero it is easy to imagine they always were. But many of us don't realise our power until we start to use it.

Lutfun Hussain lives in slightly run-down East London near Spitalfields and is part of a large, quite poor but very close Bangladeshi community. She still struggles a little with her English, which she finds mildly annoying considering how many speeches she has to make. But she didn't set out to make speeches; she set out to make curry. Lutfun is a great cook. And, frustrated that she couldn't buy traditional Bengali vegetables locally, she started growing them at the nearby Spitalfields City Farm. Lutfun was simply hungry for a taste of home, but a few years on she now runs the award-winning Coriander Club – a women's group dedicated to healthy living, environmental issues and fantastic food. They grow vegetables, exercise, gossip, cook, eat and campaign for green issues together. The internationally renowned Kew Gardens recently invited the women to advise them on the cultural significance of several South Asian plants. Lutfun knew she could cook (and, boy, can she cook – her food is delicious), but it turned out she could change the world too. Because one person becomes a few people, a few people become a movement, a movement becomes a social shift and then we get a happy-hero revolution.

But all this works only if you want it to, and if you believe it will make your life better.

So, what do you want from life? What would genuinely, truly make you happy? Here are some possibilities:

- People – feeling connected to your friends and family
- Play – fun, leisure and a bit of self-indulgence
- Comfort – a lovely, snug, happy home
- Security – safety and confidence
- Interests – learning and discovering more about the world
- Health – being healthy and looking good
- Freedom – enjoying your interests and living life as you choose
- Success – being respected and knowing you've done well
- Work – an interesting, well-paid, secure job
- Purpose – knowing you're doing something worthwhile
- Pride – high self-esteem and confidence
- Time – to think, plan and enjoy life

Your list might be completely different to the one above. You might have romance or the comfort of prayer on your list, or excitement, sex or shopping. You could have chocolate ice cream as the number-one thing that makes you feel fulfilled (I can respect that). There are no rules, and you know more than anyone else what makes you happy.

But how many of your happiness boxes does 'making a difference' currently tick? Does taking out the recycling make you feel free? Does saving electricity bring you closer to your family? Probably not. Which is why we need to change the way we change the world. Being a happy hero means knowing that acting and thinking differently about the future can deliver almost everything on your happiness list. That promise is for all of humanity, and for you personally.

The Five Lessons

By this point you've already had a bit of training, of course. You've got past the guards and you understand the dragon we're going to slay (and you realise that climate change is only one of the dragons out there and inside ourselves). And now you're ready to really learn the lessons of happy heroism.

To do this we're going to enter the world of psychology, and even neuroscience, and tinker at the deepest level of your brain, because your deep mindset is making you unhappy, and putting the whole world in danger. That might sound a bit melodramatic, but the reason your mindset is so destructive is quite simple: for the vast majority of human history our mindsets evolved to adapt us to an environment that didn't change much. For a child born into a prehistoric hunter-gatherer tribe, the rules were simple: consume everything you can (especially fats) because you must hunt or search for all your calories, and tomorrow you could starve; throw anything away because everything you use or eat is natural and will just rot anyway; be concerned about your status – adorn your body and display your wealth because these are genuinely good ways to choose a mate; do what everyone around you does because that's how small communities stay together; sit and rest as much as possible because hunting and gathering guarantees enough exercise; and be wary of outsiders – anyone different might be a threat. Within the context of these rules, the hunter-gatherers' mindset would have served them well.

But pop that same child out in the middle of a busy modern city and they will probably become obese (there are more sugars and fats available than our ancient mental programming is set up for); they'll be hung up about their body image and working to distraction to pay for overengineered status symbols; they'll throw away mountains of stuff that will last longer than they will; and despite all their intelligence and rationality, that mindset will drive that one person to consume and pollute to a level equivalent to thousands of their forebears. The same psychological responses that evolved to ensure our earliest survival are now undermining it. Our mindsets are driving us to consume, to pollute and to ignore the basic physics of living on a finite planet. They make us fat, neurotic and prejudiced against others.

But it doesn't have to be this way. We are programmed with mindsets, not specific behaviours, and with a little training you can overcome or even trick them. That's what this chapter is designed to teach you. Some of the five lessons you might find quite straightforward; others might take a lot of work. But once you master them, becoming a happy hero is easy.

So I want you to take the red pill, follow the yellow-brick road and, above all else, trust the force...

Lesson One: Know Yourself

Wouldn't the world be dull if we were all the same?

Your first lesson is to acknowledge that you are an individual, with your own interests and preferences. When it comes to being a world-saving happy hero, we all need to take on different roles, because happy heroes come in all shapes, sizes and types.

Well, three types. And it's really helpful to know which of these you are (especially when working out which actions you'd prefer to take) and, even more importantly, to know which type your friends, colleagues and audiences are when you are talking to them about how amazing the future will be!

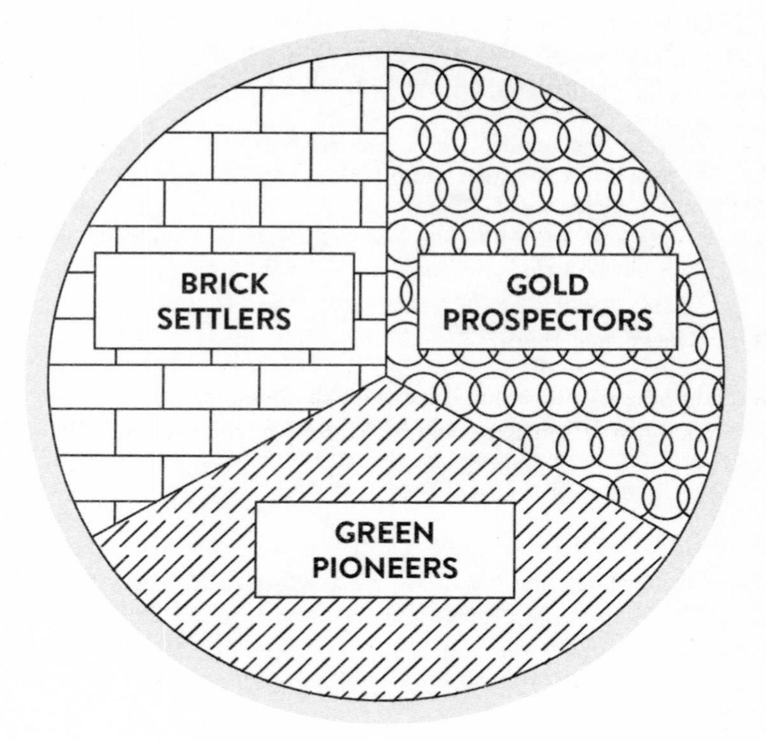

This simple typology was developed by Pat Dade, a wonderful American, partial to bear hugs and loud laughs. He has spent decades honing the scientific underpinning to this Values Modes Typology, in which he has named the three groups Pioneer, Prospector and Settler. But I kept getting them mixed up, so he gave me permission to rename them Green, Gold and Brick for the purposes of this book. The Gold/Prospector type is the largest segment, usually making up 40–60 per cent of any population, with the Green/Pioneer type next at 30–40 per cent and Brick/Settler being the smallest at 20–30 per cent. Depending on where in the world you are, those numbers can change, but you're always more likely to meet more Gold types than the others.

- **The Greens** are interested in the bigger picture and worldwide issues. They like change, new questions and

novel solutions. They are very clear on what's right and wrong, and value social justice and equality. They are often cautiously optimistic about the future and interested in environmental and social causes.
- **The Bricks** put their family and home at the centre of their world. They prefer things to be 'normal' and are suspicious of the 'latest fad'. They are wary of crime and support punishment for wrongdoing. They respect tradition and caring for the community. They are worried about the future and question the current rate of change.
- **The Golds** are excited by success and being the best at what they are doing. They welcome opportunities to show their abilities and enjoy looking good. They follow fashion and celebrities and like new ideas and novel experiences. They are optimistic about the future and search for opportunities and advancements.

Another way to see these three is as 'archetypes'. We meet all of these people in our lives, and we weave these personalities into our stories. They all take important roles and balance each other out. That's why some of our favourite fiction seems to include the three typologies, learning to work together for the greater good:

GREENS	BRICKS	GOLDS
Frodo	Sam	Merry and Pippin
Luke and Leia	C3PO	Han Solo
Woody	Hamm and Rex	Buzz Lightyear
Lisa Simpson	Marge Simpson	Bart Simpson

If you're like me, then you'll see parts of yourself in all three (I'm a Green who adores new shoes in a very Gold way). Or you might be amazed that everyone isn't your type. It can be helpful to think about your family, friends and co-workers. Perhaps you can appreciate a little more why they don't always like what you like or think what you think – they are just different types.

But don't fall into the trap of thinking that Bricks are older people or that Golds are more likely to be teenagers. The types cut across age, gender, race and all demographics.

If you're not sure which type you are, try the questionnaire below:

The phrases I most associate myself with are (tick only the **10 boxes** that apply most to you when answering this question):

C Self-improvement

B Being a winner

C Seeking justice for others

A Feeling normal

C Blending the new and the traditional

A Being part of the community

C Living 'in the now'

B Trying something a bit different

B Following celebrities' lives and lifestyles

C Helping children to be themselves

C Authenticity

B Having fun

C Doing my own thing

A Looking after the basics of home, money and food

B Shopping, fashion and looking good

C Living ethically

A Doing my duty

C Connecting with different people

B Looking and feeling my best

A Being loyal

B Bending the rules

A Learning the lessons of the past

B Being successful

C Making my own choices

B Bettering myself and getting ahead

C Questioning things and asking better questions

A Avoiding risky decisions

B Looking to the future

C Discovering, innovating and experimenting

B Making things bigger and better

C Caring for the environment and for others

A Putting family first

____

B Following trends

____

____

____

Total A________ Total B________ Total C________

____

____

Remember: you're only ticking the 10 phrases that resonate most with you, no more. Add up the ticks for each letter:

- Mainly As – you're a Brick
- Mainly Bs – you're a Gold
- Mainly Cs – you're a Green

Your answers will probably reveal a mixture of predominantly two types, and one type you're not similar to at all. Knowing your type – and other people's – will help you to pick the right behaviours and find other happy heroes who understand your way of seeing the world. And the best bit about having different types is that *you* don't have to do everything! You can leave some things to other types, while doing what feels right, right now, for you.

In the past, traditional environmentalists have mainly spoken to the Green type. Or maybe they assume that we'll all turn into Green if they talk to us as if we were. But we're not, and in fact those of you reading this book are more likely to be Gold types than any other. There are Green heroes, Gold heroes and Brick heroes. When you look around the world, you realise we need all types to make saving the world normal, cool and authentic.

The Brick Hero's Action Plan

As a Brick, you look for sensible actions that will save money, protect your community and keep your family safe. You are probably already saving energy at home (lights left on unnecessarily just seems foolish to you). You might not be trying to save the world, but you are prepared to do your bit. Every suggestion below is designed to either save you money, improve your family's health or make your community a safer and smarter place. And I hope this list will also call to mind other ideas you've had. (I find that Bricks usually already have a lot of knowledge and ideas about improving their homes and cutting waste.)

- Install an energy meter at home to reveal which appliances are using too much power.
- Join local community groups working to improve your neighbourhood's air quality, cycle routes or recycling provision.
- Grow your own food at home or in an allotment.
- Buy local food from farms or a market to support small businesses.
- Keep chickens, if you have a garden (they can thrive, even in cities).
- Sort the recycling properly, including the plastic bottles from the bathroom (which a lot of people forget).
- Switch to a renewable/green electricity tariff; some are cheaper than the standard ones and they all help to cut air pollution.
- Set up a water butt to capture rainwater from the roof for watering your garden, if you have one.
- Join the local park groups to help with the gardening and upkeep of community spaces.
- Join a neighbourhood welcome scheme to help integrate newcomers into your community and teach them about the area.
- Raise money for local charities through sponsorship, bake sales and community events.
- Find a way to volunteer and check on the most vulnerable people in your neighbourhood.
- Mend everything you can, rather than throwing things away (the internet is full of smart tips for fixing everything from torn clothes to scratched bathtubs).
- Insulate your home – roof, windows and especially cavity walls (which allow heat to leak out).
- Compost all your waste food and scraps.
- Draught-proof your home – around doors, windows and especially the garage, if you have one.

- Find a local tool-share scheme rather than spending on tools you don't use that often.
- Learn a skill like dressmaking or machine repair to keep what you have for longer.
- Take a reusable bag when you're out shopping.
- Join an energy cooperative to buy cheap solar or wind energy and free yourself from the energy companies' price hikes.
- Ask your local school, church or employer about energy saving and recycling.
- Meet local politicians and ask about how they are keeping your area green and clean (remember, they work for you).
- Vote for local politicians who will protect and conserve the environment.

All these actions and many more are simply smart ways to look after our loved ones, our homes and each other. Sometimes local politicians and businesses need a prod in the right direction, and it's easier to do that if you know you've done everything you can personally. Changing the world starts at home, with strong foundations and smart decisions.

The Gold Hero's Action Plan

As a Gold, you have an unrivalled ability to make happy heroism desirable. You know what people want, what they are talking about and what gets listened to. And, most importantly, you know how to have fun. And that's what the world needs right now: ways to make making a difference fun. You may already have tipped an ice bucket over your head or posted a no-make-up selfie. Big, bold action doesn't scare you if it's for a good cause.

All the actions suggested below are designed to get you out there, doing what you are good at. You're going to have fun, you're going to make friends and you're going to feel great.

- Discover the newest green and ethical brands – look for the Fairtrade, Organic and FSC labels.
- Host a 'Swishing' party (see later in the chapter and check out swishing.org).

- Buy an electric or hybrid car, and work your way up to the newest Tesla!
- Take the train for long journeys rather than driving; it provides perfect 'me time' relaxation.
- Book an innovative 'glamping' or 'staycation' holiday, rather than flying to all the usual places (check out Sawdays online, if you're in the UK).
- Search out unique vintage clothes and furniture.
- Buy fashion with true quality and style, rather than the trashy stuff that's worn once and then thrown away, and join the Fashion Revolution Day online every April.
- Find a local clothes repair shop (often in dry-cleaning stores) and have all your favourite looks refreshed, taken up or taken in.
- Cancel your gym membership and buy a bike instead (that way you're more likely to need those clothes taken in!)
- Improve your diet, weight and skin by cutting down on meat.
- Switch to a renewable/green electricity tariff online – and then post and share what you've done, to inspire others to do the same.
- Adopt a polar bear or buy a hectare of rainforest as an unusual gift.
- Organise a big Earth Hour party (check out earthhour.org).
- Help to make some noise online through all your channels, sharing great green products and commenting on posts about changing the world (remember, everything you post and share matters).
- Have the latest solar panels fitted, if you can afford them.
- Buy healthy organic green food and clothes for your kids.
- Make up games at home for recycling and smart energy behaviours, with a leader board or rewards.
- Comment on your favourite brands' social-media pages and tell them you want greener and more climate-friendly versions of their products.
- Speak up about what you want for the future – you're on the winning team here, so let people know it.
- Vote for people who care about people and the planet.

Following the suggestions on this list will help you to be healthier and happier, and will connect you with people and enable you to have more fun. And remember how important your voice is. Politicians and businesses really care about what matters to Golds, so let them know. This list is just your starting point. Every day new ideas and smart products are being launched: visit thehappyhero.org to find and share them.

The Green Hero's Action Plan

You probably already know what do to, so consider this list just a reminder. Of the three types, you are probably already doing the most, but may be finding the 'optimism and positivity' part of happy heroism the hardest to master. The doom section in the previous chapter might have felt familiar because Greens often carry equal amounts of guilt and anger around. But I do believe that Greens have an incredible ability to make a difference, and a true acceptance of what is needed. All I ask is that, in addition to the action list you've probably already made for yourself, you add an action from below that doesn't feel like a sacrifice. For the sake of experiment, pick one simply for the sheer pleasure of doing it!

- Phone or write to a politician right now, setting out your expectations of action.
- Find out about schemes and incentives to install the right renewables at home.
- Go fully vegetarian or vegan for a month (if you haven't already).
- Finally ditch the car completely and commit to cycling and public transport.
- Make a donation (if you can afford it) to the legal teams protecting people and the planet's rights: legal challenges are proving very effective, but are underfunded.
- If you must take them, find ways to innovatively offset flights. This can be done through the official emissions trading schemes, thereby raising the cost of emissions permits for companies.
- Start or add your name to government petitions. Many require democratic debate in Parliament or Congress if they reach a certain level of support.

- Attend, lead and plan protests – creative dissent makes waves.
- Car share everywhere.
- Find ways to defend small and local businesses.
- Buy products with the highest environmental and social credentials – check online listings and reports.
- Avoid buying stuff at all – upcycle instead.
- Ask for the 'sustainability report' for your place of work and, if it doesn't exist, ask why not.
- Calculate your carbon footprint – you might be surprised.
- Start a green group in your school, workplace or community – there may be more Greens around you than you realised.
- Fill out customer surveys at the bottom of receipts and online to demand sustainable action from businesses – they do get read.
- Write directly to CEOs of large companies, addressed to their headquarters – they also get read.
- Make a commitment to visit national parks, museums and preservation areas to show they are valued.
- Turn up at political events, shareholder meetings and community groups to raise issues like climate change.
- Vote for, work for or stand as a green politician.
- Congratulate, celebrate or thank someone who is only just starting to make a difference.

That final bullet point might be the hardest for you. If we're going to change the world, we need everyone, not just the Greens, to take action. If someone in your family or community who isn't naturally a Green starts to do something, then they deserve to hear, 'That's great. In fact, you've inspired me to do more myself. Thanks!' rather than, 'That's great, but you know it won't make any real difference unless you do this, this and this as well.' As Greens, we need to try some cheerleading alongside our criticism.

Write Your Own Plan

The actions listed above are those most suited to your type, but they're neither exclusive nor exhaustive. If you're a Brick who wants a solar panel to make your home self-sufficient, that's great. Golds can get politically active, and Greens can buy eco-fashion. But I want it to be as easy as possible for you to start, and picking something that fits your personality is more likely to work.

So now it's time to make your own list, if you haven't already. It only takes a few minutes to jot down a quick list of the next actions you could take. Then look at it and see what appeals the most. Choose one thing that you quite fancy doing anyway – not to save the planet, not because you feel guilty about it, but because you like the sound of it and think you would enjoy it – and that's where you should start. Do that one thing, see how it feels, and then choose another one.

You don't have to take on everything at once; in fact, it's better if you don't. Start small and just take the first step. This was the secret of Nobel Prize-winner Muhammad Yunus, the founder of microfinance and microlending. Before he retired, Yunus helped thousands of people in poverty obtain business loans without collateral. He started with just $27.

Yunus surveyed people in his community about their needs and was shocked to learn that he could help over 40 people by lending just $27 of his own money to buy a goat or a piece of farming equipment. His first project was a success and he continued to build on it, finally creating Grameen Bank. By 1997, Grameen had issued $6.38 billion to 7.4 million borrowers, empowering some of the poorest people to build businesses and improve their own situations.

I've found that simply having a specific goal is likely to make you happier, so just by creating your personal action plan you might start to feel better. Dr Melanie Rudd at the University of Houston reviewed six studies involving nearly 500 different people, and found that happiness was raised irrespective of whether a goal was big or small, or designed to benefit one other person or the whole world.[1]

One Big Team

Finding out about ourselves is interesting, but this lesson is also designed to teach us to appreciate the gifts and interests of others.

1. Melanie Rudd and Jennifer Aaker, 'How to Be Happy by Giving to Others', *Scientific American*, n.p., 7 July 2014.

Which segment did you tick the fewest boxes for? Go back and reread the section on the type you are least like. Then try to identify someone in your life who is that type. Reflect on what is great about that person and how they can be a happy hero too. Then think about how you might motivate them, even if their personality is different from yours. What actions in this book would they be most attracted to? What would encourage them to start taking positive action? Appreciating others' gifts can avoid a lot of arguments about climate change, or anything else for that matter. If your brother-in-law is a Brick and you are a Green, there is probably no point arguing with him about global climate injustice because that's not how he sees the world. But the value of energy independence, how efficiency can save money and the need for more local green spaces for healthier kids – these are motivating for him.

We heroes need heroes! We all have different roles and superpowers, and we need to support each other in using them. This might be the hardest part of being a hero because we all struggle sometimes to see the world through others' eyes. But 'welcoming' is a good word whatever type you are. We're all in this together – Bricks, Golds and Greens. And we're going to need to cheerlead each other up that curve to the big rewards.

Lesson Two: Believe in Yourself

Did you know that Walt Disney was fired by a newspaper editor who said he 'lacked imagination'? Or that Thomas Edison tried and failed a thousand times before he invented the light bulb? And how did the resolute Edison respond to his repeated failures? 'I didn't fail 1,000 times,' he said. 'The light bulb was an invention with 1,000 steps.'

Thomas Edison is a perfect illustration of our second goal in happy heroism: self-belief, or what psychologists call 'agency'.

Agency is a measure of your belief in your own ability to affect the world around you – that you have free will and can have some control over life. It's shocking how few people believe that, which is a pity, because knowing you can affect things is very good for you. I don't mean shouting at the TV and thinking it will make your team score more goals, but knowing that your opinions and actions will make a difference in your life and in the lives of others.

No one is born with a high sense of agency. When we're little kids we don't have much free will; the adults around us make our decisions and we often don't have a clue what's going on. But we grow up and we have kids of our own. We know we can make a difference to them, and we hope we can make the world a little better, safer and more fun for them, too.

One of my favourite happy heroes is Helen Keller. Born in 1880 in Alabama, she was a perfectly normal child for the first 18 months of her life – crying and cooing, learning to recognise her parents' voices and faces, smiling at other children. 'Then', as she recalled later, 'came the illness which closed my eyes and ears and plunged me into the unconsciousness of a new-born baby.' No one knows what illness afflicted her, although some modern scholars suspect it was meningitis. Whatever it was, it left her both deaf and blind, and because she'd been too young to learn before the illness struck, she also couldn't speak.

As she grew she became wild. She would kick out at her family and throw herself around. Many of her relatives were convinced she should be institutionalised – all too common for anyone suffering disability in those times.

But her family persevered and found a wonderful teacher called Anne Sullivan, who was herself partially deaf. Sometimes having to physically restrain her charge, Anne slowly taught Helen to understand how to connect words spelled out on her palm to real objects and feelings.

Despite such a difficult start and lifelong health challenges, Helen went on to become one of the leading voices for disability and women's rights in America and, indeed, the world. As she said of her vocation: 'Helping your fellow men were one's only excuse for being in this world and in the doing of things to help one's fellows lay the secret of lasting happiness.'

She travelled to over 40 different countries giving motivational speeches, met US presidents and was friends with many famous figures, including Alexander Graham Bell, Charlie Chaplin and Mark

Twain. Twain declared: 'The two most interesting characters of the nineteenth century are Napoleon and Helen Keller.' Helen was controversial, proud and opinionated, despite never regaining her ability to hear or see, and she left great wisdom for those happy heroes following in her footsteps:

> I slip back many times: I fall, I stand still. I run against the edge of hidden obstacles. I lose my temper and find it again, and keep it better. I trudge on, I gain a little. I feel encouraged. I get more eager and climb higher and begin to see widening horizons.[2]

Helen Keller teaches us that we can all have agency over our lives, though not without effort, and sometimes in the face of great challenges. But that promise is given to us all.

And the alternative isn't pleasant. People with low agency are those who think that fate, destiny or powerful people dictate their lives, and studies show there is a higher incidence of violence among them and that they are more antisocial.[3] And why wouldn't they be? If you have such a low opinion of your own ability to change things, then nothing you do matters. Conspiracy theories are born here. Excuses for bad behaviour and addictions find fertile ground when agency is low.

It shocks me how many people have lost their sense of agency and forgotten how powerful they are. Some potential heroes don't just doubt their ability to affect big things like climate change; they don't even feel in control of their own lives or decisions. And that can become a self-fulfilling prophecy, because when we have low agency we don't try as hard, we pay less attention and we can be taken advantage of more easily. Low agency seriously sucks. We need to learn how much control we really have.

2. Alden Whitman, 'Helen Keller, 87, Dies', *New York Times*, 2 June 1968: n.p. On This Day (web).

3. K. Kwak and A. Bandura, 'Role of Perceived Self-Efficacy and Moral Disengagement in Antisocial Conduct', manuscript (1998) (Osan College, Seoul, Korea).

People Power

Right now the idealists reading this will be punching the air. But the realists might be raising a sardonic eyebrow and thinking: 'Really? Can normal people truly make a difference to huge things like climate change?'

The power of positive action can be compelling, but taking it all the way to believing that we have the agency to change the world can be a much harder leap. It's tempting to wait for governments or businesses to take the lead.

I work with CEOs and elected officials every day. While some are genuinely trying to improve their companies or countries, many of their initiatives are going to take a long while to take effect. Trying to change big companies or whole countries is like trying to turn a massive cruise ship: even if you know which direction you want to move it in (i.e. away from the iceberg), it can take a while to alter its course.

But when it comes to climate change in particular, your actions matter as much as those of businesses or governments, perhaps even more so. That might come as a surprise, but remember: people power has always had the potential to be more important than powerful people.

Research that I commissioned for this book shows that average folk in the UK could cut the country's carbon footprint by 50 per cent. Together we could do this, just by making a few adaptations to what we were going to do anyway. You don't hear much about this potential because even those working to make positive change often overlook the smaller things, focusing instead on the big things that governments could do.

Imagine, for a moment, someone's face lit up by her computer screen. She is doing what 4 million people in the UK do every single year – changing her energy supplier online, a common, normal thing that many of us have done on a switching site. But now imagine that she is changing to a renewable energy supplier. That's a bit more difficult as today only 3 per cent of us choose to buy our electricity from a green supplier, but ask for some extra effort from your imagination and see her clicking on the green-energy tariff.

Remember, she is one of 4 million British people who are changing their provider *anyway*, that year; she is part of the natural transition from one energy supplier to another. However, if she simply made a greener choice, then we've got one little pebble in a possible landslide. It helps to remember that many green-energy tariffs cost the same as non-green ones, and sometimes they can even be cheaper. They work by matching the energy you take out of the grid with energy put in from wind turbines, solar panels and hydro power (which is all getting cheaper to generate every year).

Our lady is just one person, but this is where it gets interesting. If only half the people who change suppliers in one year switched to a renewables tariff, it would increase demand for green energy by 835 per cent. The strain on current green-energy supplies would be too much, as the energy companies would need to produce 20 per cent more renewable energy in one year than the entire UK currently produces. There would be a crisis, national media outrage and probably illegal deals online. The pressure on the government to reassess future energy demand would be massive and the resultant kerfuffle would be very interesting, to say the least. No extra taxes would be needed and no 'incentives' for energy companies to do the right thing – because demand would drive private investment. One little click could transform everything, from the bottom up.

And energy is only the start. Imagine if all the cars that were bought in a single year were greener or electric cars (their sales are soaring so fast that might be inevitable, anyway). Or if we all cut our weekly meat consumption a little bit?

Intrigued by this idea, I asked the research team to take their analysis a step further. They found that if you took an average day in the UK's purchases of new cars, energy tariffs, food and holidays, and turned those into green purchases, then 250,000 tonnes of carbon emissions would be saved. That's how much a coal-fired power station pumps out every year. That means that together, we could turn off a highly polluting, coal-fired power station for a whole year just by changing our personal choices for one day. Imagine that, just from people buying products they were intending to buy anyway. No government, pressure group or business could achieve so much in one day.

Of course, it wouldn't be that simple. The infrastructure isn't there. The economy isn't set up for such a change at such a speed. But I'd like to see how governments and businesses would scramble to keep up if our choices turned into positive action. Rather than hoping for leadership, we'd force it upon our leaders, with all excuses and delays being swept away. I'd very much like to see that day.

If you've ever felt small, remember all this. This is the sheer scale of what you can do. It is the scale of your agency. And simply believing in yourself does work. In tests, people who believe that throughout their lives they can keep learning and raise their aptitude performed far better in intelligence tests than those who thought they couldn't.[4] So regardless of your original IQ, believing you can raise it makes you perform better. Researchers also tested successful entrepreneurs to see what makes them succeed.[5] They suspected these people were driven by a need to achieve and prove themselves, but were surprised to find that they actually scored rather low on 'need for achievement'. What the entrepreneurs did have in common, however, was a belief in themselves – a high sense of agency and a knowledge that they can change things.

The benefits pile up. People who believe they can improve their own health, even in cases of serious illness like cancer and diabetes, can show improvements.[6] That's an extraordinary finding. Doctors discovered this phenomenon in controlled trials with thousands of

4. J. S. Moser, H. S. Schroder, C. Heeter, T. P. Moran and Y.-H. Lee, 'Mind Your Errors: Evidence for a Neural Mechanism Linking Growth Mind-Set to Adaptive Posterror Adjustments', *Psychological Science*, 22.12 (2011): 1484–9.

5. Ove C. Hansemark, 'Need for Achievement, Locus of Control and the Prediction of Business Start-Ups: A Longitudinal Study,' *Journal of Economic Psychology*, 24.3 (2003): 301–19.

6. Two examples: (1) Jason Van Allen, Ric G. Steele, Michael B. Nelson, James Peugh, Anna Egan, Mark Clements and Susana R. Patton, 'A Longitudinal Examination of Hope and Optimism and Their Role in Type 1 Diabetes in Youths, *Journal of Pediatric Psychology*, 41.7 (2015): 741–9. (2) Melanie Price et al., 'Helplessness/Hopelessness, Minimization and Optimism Predict Survival in Women with Invasive Ovarian Cancer: A Role for Targeted Support During Initial Treatment Decision-Making?' *Supportive Care in Cancer*, 24.6 (2016): 2627–34.

people. So, rather than just testing drugs, there are now medical programmes investigating how to raise patients' sense of agency over their health. From being more likely to stick to a diet or take up exercise to giving up smoking,[7] a positive, high-agency brain is a massive advantage in life. As Mahatma Gandhi said: 'If I have the belief that I can do it, I shall surely acquire the capacity to do it, even if I may not have it at the beginning.'

Albert Bandura of Stanford University has done a great deal of the breakthrough research on this self-efficacy and agency, studying what you need to do in order to grow that sense of self-belief.[8] Here are four exercises based on Dr Bandura's work that will help to build your sense of agency (and enjoy the benefits that come with it):

1. **When have you made something happen?** The most effective way to grow your sense of agency is to remind yourself that you've made a difference before – because success breeds success. Write down three things you have managed to achieve in your life (perhaps even despite difficulties or setbacks). If you're struggling to reach a list of three, then do one of the actions from your Green, Brick or Gold hero's action plan and you've got one! It's healthy to keep adding to your list of action/achievement/success over time. It doesn't matter if each point is large or small, because you're simply reminding yourself that you have a proven track record of making things happen. It's a wonderful feeling to make this list. I highly recommend it.
2. **Can you find role models?** Another great way to raise your sense of agency is to find people like you who have already done it. You can read about some on our happy-hero website. And there are many books and movies about real people who have made a difference (the movie *Erin Brockovich* is one of my favourites). Think about the attributes and mindsets those role models have, and think about how you can be more like them. This is called

7. A. Luszczynska and R. Schwarzer, 'Social Cognitive Theory', in M. Conner and P. Norman (Eds), *Predicting Health Behaviour*, vol. 2, pp. 127–69 (Buckingham, UK: Open University Press, 2005).

8. Albert Bandura, 'Self-Efficacy', in V. S. Ramachaudran (Ed.), *Encyclopedia of Human Behavior*, vol. 4, pp. 71–81 (New York: Academic Press, 1994).

'modelling success' and it's a great way to overcome personal blockages to agency.

3. **What do people think of you?** People might see you as stronger and more able than you think. Ask your friends, family and colleagues to drop you a note about your top three strengths and/or an example of where you made a difference in their lives. Offer to return the favour, if they'd like you to. Then believe in their feedback with as much conviction as you'd apply to their criticism. Keep a note of those strengths and commit to use them more to make a difference in your own and other people's lives.

4. **Are you stressed or are you excited?** Here's a helpful trick: rename 'stress' as 'excitement' in your head. For example, you're about to make a speech and you're feeling anxious and agitated, with sweaty palms and a racing heart. If you say out loud (or even to yourself), 'Wow, I must be really excited about this speech!' it can reset your brain. Even though it's a trick you're playing on your own mind, reframing problems as signs of success can transform your agency. It's the same when you're exercising: when your muscles ache, rather than viewing this as an indication of how out of shape you are, think of every ache and twinge as a sign that the exercise is working and building strength. With high agency difficulties become challenges to be mastered.

This can all become self-reinforcing. The more you think you can achieve something, the harder you are likely to work at it. The alternative is giving up, or assuming you don't have what it takes, which guarantees failure. And anyway, the fact you're reading this book proves to me that you do believe in yourself, even if just a little. And sometimes a little is all you need.

Do you remember the children's story *The Little Engine That Could*? The little engine set out on its seemingly impossible journey to pull a long train over a high mountain, repeating, 'I think I can, I think I can, I think I can,' all the way. And it did.

Lesson Three: Have Fun

If you're sitting comfortably, then let me tell you a story (well, two).

Story 1

Once upon a time, a vaguely green-minded princess stood staring at her recycling bin. She heaved a deep sigh and tried not to think about what all those wine bottles said about her lifestyle. There was no room for any more bottles and, for one fleeting moment, the princess considered dumping the lot in her normal bin. 'But no,' she thought righteously, 'I'm a decent person. I'll take this to the recycling bins.'

She scrabbled around under the sink and found some shopping bags to fill with bottles, slung them in the back of the car (she'd meant to walk, but realised there were too many bottles for that) and drove five minutes to the municipal recycling point. She left the car running and jumped out to pop the wine bottles into the bins. Left with the plastic bags smelling of stale wine, she stuffed them between the bins (as several people before her had done), jumped back in the car and drove home to wash her hands. 'I'm glad I won't have to do that again for a while,' the princess sighed as she reached for the corkscrew.

Story 2

Once upon a time, the daughter of a vaguely green-minded princess started tugging on her mother's arm and begging: 'Please can we do the recycling? Pleeeeease?'

'Oh well,' sighed the princess with a smile, 'we've already been this week, but OK.' The princess grabbed one bottle, while her daughter hugged the other to her. They walked for a few minutes to the municipal recycling point. The ground was painted green and the bins themselves were white with black blotches on them.

'Lift me up, lift me up, I wanna do it,' squealed the princess's daughter.

As the first bottle plopped into the bin there was an audible 'mooooo'.

With a satisfied little sigh, the princess's daughter proudly declared: 'I love feeding the cows.'

The moral? Fun works.

In both stories the action is exactly the same. The recycling isn't any easier or any closer to home. A bottle goes in a bin. The only difference is a lick of paint and a cow-noise gizmo that took the recycling behaviour off the worthy 'to-do' list and put it instead on the 'pleasure, leisure and fun' list. Unsurprisingly, it's the second list that's more likely to get done. Well done to London councils for making this story a reality.

When you read through the lists of actions earlier some of them probably seemed easy or rewarding, while others looked more worthy or boring. That's OK – start with whichever ones you want. But at some point you might want to push yourself to do even more and take on some of the seemingly less desirable actions. The question then is: How can they be rewarding too? And my answer? Find a way to make them fun.

We are all programmed to seek fun, leisure, fulfilment, entertainment, novelty, indulgence, humour and silliness. Collectively, researchers refer to that list as 'pleasure'. And making changing the world a pleasure is what this book is all about.

The Neuroscience of Pleasure

Pleasure is made up of two ingredients: one can be tracked down in the brain and even stimulated with electrodes; the other is a bit harder to pinpoint but, thankfully, comes guaranteed just by being a happy hero. The first is called 'hedonic' and the second 'eudemonic'.

I'm going to rename hedonic as 'feeling' and eudemonic as 'meaning'. People who experience both claim to be the happiest people on earth.[9] The 'feeling' type of pleasure is often signalled to the brain from the senses and could include a lovely taste, a beautiful view, a fast run, a glass of wine, a cuddle from your child, an illegal drug, a snog or laughing at a movie. All these experiences light up simi-

9. Richard M. Ryan and Edward L. Deci, 'On Happiness and Human Potentials: A Review of Research on Hedonic and Eudemonic Well-Being', *Annual Review of Psychology*, 52.1 (2001): 141–66.

lar parts of your brain. Different people might enjoy some of these much more than others, but all of them are hedonic 'feeling' pleasures. Think about when you have enjoyed the most feeling pleasure in the last few days or weeks. Remember that this needs to be a feeling from your senses – from your body. It's really helpful to know what lights up the 'feeling hotspots' in your own brain if you're going to try to make being green fun. Chocolate features heavily in my list.

In the 1950s, psychologists James Olds and Peter Milner implanted electrodes in these 'pleasure centres' of rats' brains.[10] They then put a lever in the animals' cage which, when the rats pressed it, gave their electrodes a buzz. The rats pressed that pleasure lever as many as 7,000 times per hour. They preferred pleasure-circuit stimulation to food (even when they were hungry) and water (even when they were thirsty). Male rats would ignore a female in heat and even cross painful electrified floor grids to reach the lever; females would abandon their newborn pups to continually press it. Some rats would self-stimulate as often as 2,000 times per hour for 24 hours, to the exclusion of all other activities. A few of them had to be unhooked from the electrodes to prevent death by self-starvation. Pressing that lever became their entire world. The results of this experiment became one of the most infamous in the history of neuroscience.

Imagine harnessing even a tiny percentage of that power to make changing the world easier – not by using electrodes, but by finding ways to make making a difference an absolute pleasure in itself.

And we humans can make our feeling pleasures even more powerful, because unlike rats, we are at our happiest when our powerful 'feeling' pleasure is matched with 'meaning' (or eudemonic) pleasure. You experience these meaning pleasures when something you do is worthwhile in your own eyes.

Following a lecture on mental health, the famous psychiatrist Dr Karl Menninger was once asked: 'What would you advise a person to do, if they felt a nervous breakdown coming on?' Most people thought he would say: 'Consult a psychiatrist.' But he surprised every-

10. James Olds and Peter Milner, 'Pleasure Centers in the Brain', *Science America*, 195 (n.d.): 105–16.

one when he replied: 'Leave your house, find someone in need and do something to help that person.'

That's meaning pleasure: the sense that your actions have a purpose. And for human beings, meaning can generate a truly deep sense of satisfaction and fulfilment. All those sensual feeling pleasures are still fun without meaning pleasure, of course. Anyone who has guiltily eaten a chocolate cake knows it can still be pleasurable. And a worthwhile meaning experience without feeling pleasure can be hard to enjoy. Anyone who's eaten a rice cake rather than a chocolate one gets that. Feeling pleasure is the gatekeeper to action, because we are all wired for it. Those people who are able to live their lives on meaning pleasure alone, denying their feeling pleasure, we call saints!

The fact that humans need both feeling and meaning pleasure is great for us happy heroes. We already know that saving the world is meaningful. We know that doing what we can to cut carbon, help other people and make it around the crisis curve is probably the most meaningful thing we can be doing right now. The problem with saving the world has never been a lack of meaning, but rather a distinct lack of feeling, and our happy-hero rule is that every action should be rewarded. So how do we bring more feeling to our meaning?

Playing at It

A mother watches her nine-month-old baby. She smiles at him and brings her hands slowly up to cover her eyes. '*Uphi? Uphi?* [Where? Where?]' she asks. The baby stares at the mother's hands, with a little smile spreading as the anticipation builds for a few seconds. '*Na-a-a-a-a-n hut!* [Here!]' she laughs, uncovering her eyes on the '*hut*' and grinning, as her little child laughs with pleasure. The language is Xhosa, a Bantu click language, and the scene is being played out in a mud-walled hut in a rural village in South Africa. The words and the vocal melody of the game are different in Xhosa and English, but the rhythm, rules and sheer joy in the inevitable outcome are similar across the world. This description comes from one of the many research studies into Peek-a-Boo.[11] The game has been studied by psychologists since the 1920s as one of the best and most global examples of a deep human need: to play.

Play is everywhere because it drives us to explore new things, stretch our abilities, learn and adapt. Sadly, before long, adulthood sneaks up on us. We stop 'playing', and the very phrase 'playing games' can take on exasperating connotations. Until recently, that is.

The thumb-numbingly addictive game Angry Birds has now been downloaded over a billion times. (To put that in context, only 275 million copies of Monopoly have been sold since it was created in the early 1900s.) As a measure of how powerful play can be, in just one week of playing World of Warcraft I reached the dizzying heights of 'Level 10 Paladin', but had to cancel my subscription in order to get some sleep.

I'm not saying we need a computer game designed to save the world (although if you're designing one, then thank you). But we can learn a lot from how games work, not least because the actual behaviours the majority of games use are even more boringly repetitive than most green ones. That might sound strange if you're an enthralled gamer, but watch someone when they are playing a computer game. As many exasperated parents and partners have found, it looks quite dull from the outside – repeatedly pressing a button, moving a piece, staring at a screen. Yet games manage to take a behaviour that would become achingly dull within moments and turn it into a means of activating a whole world of fun. How they do that is called 'gamification'.

Companies have been using gamification for a long time. Supermarkets that offer loyalty cards, gyms and fitness regimes that provide badges for achievement, and big businesses that award bonuses for hitting targets all use gamification to motivate people.

Using gaming to help save the world is called 'Gamification for Good'. A great example is the 'Deep Bin' project. An experiment sponsored by Volkswagen,[12] the deep bin is a normal bin placed in a park which suffers from litter problems. But it is fitted with a movement-activated speaker, so that when you drop even a small piece of litter into it – say, a used can – it makes a sound like a huge, heavy

11. Kevin B. MacDonald, *Parent–Child Play Descriptions and Implications* (Albany, NY: State University of New York Press, 1993).

12. *The Fun Theory*, n.p., 21 September 2009. Web: 4 April 2017, thefuntheory.com.

object is falling for miles down, with a big crash and boom when it hits the bottom. Videos of the smart bin *in situ* show children (and adults) scouring the park for litter in order to activate the deep-drop sound.

Nissan used similar thinking to design their NissanConnect telematics system, which keeps track of and displays information for drivers. Now a Nissan Leaf is already quite innovative – it's an electric car, after all. But Leaf drivers also have a 7-inch screen that tracks their energy-usage information and allows them to see daily, monthly and annual reports showing distances travelled and total and average energy consumption. It also compares them to other Leaf drivers. As a Leafer, you are in competition with all the other Leafers and can pursue badges and rewards for being a smart driver.

The Rewards of Fun

Our brains are wired with what scientists refer to as 'reward pathways'. When stimulated, these pathways trigger the release of endorphins which make us feel good. Which isn't just nice, it's also crucial for our health, because when pleasure is absent, our vulnerability to stress tends to increase and our bodies release a variety of chemicals that inflame the body and result in physical irritation and disease. And there's a nasty feedback loop, because as we become more chronically stressed, our bodies have even more difficulty in fully experiencing pleasure.

Research by Professor Richard Davidson at the University of Wisconsin has shown that when the parts of your brain associated with pleasure are active, then levels of the stress hormone cortisol are reduced. So pursuing pleasure and feeling stress, it turns out, are mutually exclusive. This means that embracing pleasurable experiences may present not just an opportunity for warm fuzzies, but a very real antidote to stress and a much-needed ingredient for sustained well-being.

Just smiling or laughing also reduces those stress hormones. Not only does it make you feel good, it also lowers your blood pressure, improves breathing and regulates your heartbeat, which can counter the stress response.

Put simply: fun is very good for you.

Swish It

My business partner, Ed Gillespie, says: 'To subvert the dominant paradigm you've got to have more fun than them, and let them know it.' My favourite example of this is something my business has run for the past decade: clothes-swapping parties called Swishes.

Swishing was born out of a big argument. My business had spent years marketing green products and ideas. Everyone who works at Futerra is very committed, and debates would rage across the office about the carbon footprint of everything from cars to different brands of chocolate. Things would get very heated every sales season, because some of us loved shopping for clothes and shoe bargains, while others would remind us of the 2 million tonnes of clothing waste sent to landfill every year, the 'half a diesel car' carbon footprint of each regular shopper's annual clothes purchases and even the millions of children slaving away in fashion-supply chains. The arguments got quite heated (with Greeny Golds on one side and Greeny Bricks on the other), but rather than just shout at each other, we tried to imagine a different way of being fashionable without the footprint. And so we conjured up Swishing.

Inspired by an old idea – the yard or jumble sale – Swishing was easy once we realised it had actually been around for years, but had just lost its glamour (if it ever had any). We rebranded the jumble sale, added champagne, thought up some 'Rules of the Rail' to crank up the excitement (no scratching, biting or snatching) and even brought in some stylists and seamstresses to the most high-profile Swishes. The result? A global, fun, green phenomenon, much larger and more popular than we ever imagined. At a Swishing party you bring along 'pre-loved' clothes, jewellery and accessories. All the guests then peruse the rails (with Prosecco in hand) and try on and recommend pieces to each other. It's social shopping. At some point the hostess will declare the Swish 'open', and then you can grab the perfect thing you've had your eye on. It can get a little competitive, like a day at the sales, but it's also quite glam – all without any money being exchanged or any new clothes being manufactured. At least a quarter of my wardrobe is now Swished, and I adore the parties, with the gossip, fun, warmth and meaning of it all (not to mention the Donna Karan dress I once landed). Swishing is the perfect 'feeling-and-meaning' combination. Since our first little party, it has hit six continents, been profiled in *Vogue* and even featured in *The Archers*. Over 20,000 women are estimated to have Swished in one year alone, potentially saving hundreds of tonnes of clothing and carbon.

As Lucy Shea, Futerra's godmother of Swishing, says: 'Make it fun if you want it done.'

Lesson Four: Work Together

Holly wanted to compete in the London triathlon, which starts with a 750m swim, followed by a 20km cycle, and finishing with a 5km run that many serious competitors do at a sprint.

Most of her friends were incredulous, to put it mildly, not least because Holly was a self-professed 'couch potato' who hadn't swum, cycled or run in years. My friend Hermione Taylor first met Holly through her website The DoNation. Hermione set up The DoNation to 'help people inspire others to take action for a healthier, happier and more sustainable world'. We've all sponsored friends for charity fun runs and the like, but The DoNation is a little different, because rather than pledging money in support, you pledge to take small green actions instead. Holly had committed to the rigours of a triathlon, and in return she asked her friends to pledge to cycle to work, change to a green-energy supplier or go meat-free once a week. It's an unusual idea, but it works amazingly well. In Holly's case, hundreds of people pledged to go a little bit greener, and in return she trained and trained. It wasn't always easy, and many times she felt like quitting, but whenever she hit a wall she logged on and saw all the people who had taken action that day.

When Hermione and Holly eventually met in person, Holly burst into tears – tears of pride that she'd successfully completed such an amazing feat and that so many people had backed her by making the world a better place. What she didn't know, however, was that on that day Hermione was finding it hard to go on herself. Setting up an organisation is difficult, and the challenges involved in keeping the

DoNation website going had built up. But hearing Holly's story gave Hermione the push she needed to keep going. And today The DoNation is growing, with thousands of people pledging action.

This story is a perfect example of the old saying: 'If you want to go fast, go alone. If you want to go far, go together.'

New research is proving how much we need other people if we are planning to make a change in our lives. If you want to give up smoking, you're more likely to succeed if you're part of a friendship group doing the same. We lose weight when those around us do so. We even vote if our friends and family vote.[13] So this lesson is about how we all need each other as we face our crossroads.

The Transition Town movement was born in the small UK market town of Totnes in 2005, bringing local people together to work on ways to make their town more independent and sustainable. Buying from local shops, bringing in renewable energy, setting up allotments for people to grow their own food – each plan is built to tackle big issues like carbon and reducing oil dependence. But the daily reality is lots of people making their town a much nicer place to live in. The idea has grown apace and there are now over 1,130 transition towns registered in 43 countries around the world. I lived in Brixton, in central London, for nearly 20 years and saw the Brixton Transition Borough take off. And I still have a few 'Brixton pounds'. One of the more unexpected outcomes of transition towns, the Brixton pound (or the Stroud, Lewes or Bristol pound) is a currency that you can use to buy from local shops and producers. You can be paid in the special pounds for favours or volunteering, and then spend them in street markets and corner shops. Every time you bring one out you get a smile from locals around you because it's a sign that you care about your neighbourhood and want to keep it vibrant and resilient. It's a brilliant way of belonging.

And this is important, because we humans are social creatures who need to belong. A team at Nottingham Trent University studied how connected over 4,000 people felt to friendships, clubs, teams and other groups, and then they measured the impact this had upon their

13. D. W. Nickerson, 'Is Voting Contagious? Evidence from Two Field Experiments', *American Political Science Review*, 102(1) (2008): 49–57.

levels of happiness. They found that those who felt a strong sense of belonging to social groups were much happier.[14] There is mounting evidence that feeling accepted, welcomed or included generates positive emotions like happiness, elation, calm and satisfaction. But if we are rejected or excluded, we'll feel strong negative emotions such as anxiety, jealousy, depression and grief. The psychological pain caused by social rejection is so intense that it involves the same brain regions that are activated in the experience of physical pain. One study even found that just a single instance of exclusion can undermine our performance in an IQ test.[15]

Thankfully, connection, compassion and community are all around us. And that's how we want to work as happy heroes – building a community to support each of us as we make better lives in a better world. And there are practical tools to make that happen. One of the largest research studies on community identified the four key ingredients of successful communities.[16] Together we need to build each of these into our happy-hero movement:

- **Sense of belonging.** We need to treat each other with respect and welcome people to join our movement. Common symbols help (like the name 'happy hero'), as do having online spaces that belong to us. We need to be safe together and recognise that all happy heroes are working to make a difference – in whatever ways they choose.
- **Chance to change things.** We need to listen to each other's views and be open to influence from those ideas. The best communities change and evolve over time because the members help to develop, change and improve each other's lives.
- **Problem solving.** Our community needs to make a difference to us all. We need to help solve each other's

14. J. R. H. Wakefield, F. Sani, V. Madhok et al., 'The Relationship Between Group Identification and Satisfaction with Life in a Cross-Cultural Community Sample', *Journal of Happiness Studies* (2016): 18: 785

15. Geoff Macdonald and Mark R. Leary, 'Why Does Social Exclusion Hurt? The Relationship Between Social and Physical Pain', *Psychological Bulletin*, 131.2 (2005): 202–23.

16. D. M. Chavis, J. H. Hogge, D. W. McMillan and A. Wandersman, 'Sense of Community Through Brunswick's Lens: A First Look', *Journal of Community Psychology*, 14(1) (1986): 24–40.

problems, even if they are not the same as our own, so we will offer advice, contacts, information and support. We all need to feel that our community is valuable to us.

- **Feeling differently.** In a world of negativity our community needs to uplift and encourage. We need to build our story together and believe that the best is yet to come.

These are the principles we are going to base our movement on. But how on earth are we supposed to organise all that?

Hang on a minute. Let me just check my Facebook-Twitter-Weibo-Tumblr-Email-Orkut-Pinterest-YouTube-Instagram-(insert newest social-media channel here). How's this for lucky? Just when we needed a way of coordinating with each other… just when normal people all over the world being able to talk to each other would come in handy… and just when we need it most – we've got social media. And thankfully, everything suggested in this book can be done more easily, faster and quicker online.

Over 10 per cent of the world's population is already on Facebook. If it were a country, it would be the third largest, after China and India. About 2 billion more human beings are due to come online for the first time in the next five years. New applications, technologies and interactions are constantly being plotted in Silicon Valley, in Kenya, in Beijing and in geeks' bedrooms across the world by the light of flickering screens.

If you're online and building networks, connections, friends and communities, then you've been preparing to build this community of happy heroes. Every photo you've posted, status you've changed and joke you've shared has been your warm-up act. You've been stretching your social-media muscles and limbering up your influence hamstrings. If you've ever used social media to try to change something for the better, then you've practically reached black-belt level.

The best bit is that so have others, all over the world. The internet is spreading faster than electricity to parts of the world considered almost impossible to reach. People in Kenya, Afghanistan and Vietnam are building their own wireless networks out of wood, cans, plastic tubs, old wire and car batteries. For about $60 these MacGyvered connections can serve hundreds of people, especially in places where cautious internet companies dare not tread. In Mogadishu, over 20 per cent of the population now has access to the internet at least once a week. Remember: these new users have had ample access to holy war, in a state too dangerous for foreigners to visit freely. But they are getting online.

And all this has happened in one generation. This worldwide shift in behaviours, power, information and access began around the time I was born. The internet was invented as a way for academics to share data, and built by the US military to control operations. Email was conceived for use by the administrators of the internet to coordinate their small group. Text messaging was supposed to be a sideline to mobile calling. Facebook was going to help geeks find a date. It all sort of happened because people had the enthusiasm and vision to make it real. And now you have more computing power at your fingertips than NASA had when they put a man on the moon.

The growth of the internet is great news for us happy heroes. Firstly, because it's the ultimate tool, but also because it proves how quickly huge change can happen. We should be inspired by the speed and huge scale of change in the last few decades. But while the internet is impressive in itself, it's what we've already done with it that's really extraordinary. The content, people and connections are the good bit. And that makes you the good bit too. The technology will ramp up, link up and throw up more surprises, and the number of people online will simply grow. It will affect how we act, how we talk to each other, what we think about the world and what we think about ourselves. Considering the mindset shift we need, we couldn't have asked for a better tool.

But what do you need to do? Every day there will be something new, as we move through the crisis curve and start to climb up and over it. Smart, creative people (that's you, by the way) will build networks, apps, tags, games, platforms and a heap of cool, new, world-saving stuff. And right now, we can begin to make a community of happy heroes working to create a picture of what we want. We need to focus on the future and share our ideas of how amazing that's going to be. The millions and billions of us need to see flashes of our big payback. So…

… grab a cup of coffee and your nearest computer, tablet, phone or multi-connection online interface device and:

- **connect** to happy-hero communities online: search out people who think like you, wherever they may be, extend your networks, follow people who talk positively about the future, and remember, this is all about people, millions of wonderful, helpful, awesome people who know they are going to kick climate change's ass and win a better future together;
- **play:** this is the fun bit – you can use social media to make green actions more fun, desirable and high status, or use apps to make action more pleasurable by getting in training, talking to each other, and trying things out together and seeing if they work;
- **support:** if anyone in your online community takes a positive action, then like-like-like it; post your own tricks and ideas to help others – we are each other's cheerleader, coach, guru and prime motivator, and we need to stay motivated to keep each other motivated!

Not all happy heroes call themselves that, but you'll know them when you see them. You're welcome to start by joining thehappyhero.org. Or tag what you're doing with #happyhero so we can find you. We're all waiting to meet you.

And remember Hermione's wonderful DoNation? Well, a few years ago a girl called Pip committed to take shorter showers to help support a boy called Sham on the site. Months later, he promised to eat greener to support her Leeds 10km run. Now they are happily in love and planning a life together. You never know what might happen when you start to change the world online…

Lesson Five: Stay Optimistic

Would you like to:

- live longer and feel healthier[17]
- be happier[18]

- have a better love life[19]
- have more success at work[20]
- be liked more by other people[21]
- cope with illness more successfully[22]
- be better at solving problems[23]
- be retweeted on Twitter more often?

You would? Well you just need a little optimism.

Optimism is like healthy fruit and vegetables for the brain, whereas pessimism is a little toxin. The noted psychologist Professor Martin Seligman researched both optimists and pessimists for his book *Learned Optimism*,[24] and came up with a helpful definition: optimists tend to view anything adverse as temporary, specific and external, while pessimists will view the same situation as permanent, pervasive and personal. And these two ways of looking at the world deliver very different results in life.

Optimism is one of the defining attributes of a happy hero: feeling hopeful that the world can improve for the better and believing that the outcome of our fight against climate change will be victory. This mindset is a gift in itself and is the ultimate renewable resource. As the famous poet Alexander Pope once wrote: 'Hope springs eternal in the human breast.'

17. Eric S. Kim, Kaitlin A. Hagan, Francine Grodstein, Dawn L. DeMeo, Immaculata De Vivo and Laura D. Kubzansky, 'Optimism and Cause-Specific Mortality: A Prospective Cohort Study', *American Journal of Epidemiology*, 185(1) (2017): 21–9.

18. Martin E. P. Seligman, *Authentic Happiness: Using the New Positive Psychology to Realize Your Potential for Lasting Fulfillment* (New York: Free Press, 2002)

19. Sanjay Srivastava, Kelly M. McGonigal, Jane M. Richards, Emily A. Butler and James J. Gross, 'Optimism in Close Relationships: How Seeing Things in a Positive Light Makes Them So', *Journal of Personality and Social Psychology*, 91.1 (2016): 143–53.

20. Ron Kaniel, Cade Massey and David T. Robinson, *The Importance of Being an Optimist: Evidence from Labor Markets*, NBER Working Paper No. 16328, September 2010.

21. Martin E. P. Seligman, *Learned Optimism: How to Change Your Mind and Your Life* (New York: Vintage, 2006).

22. Harvard Health Publications, 'Optimism and Your Health', *Harvard Health*, n.p., May 2008.

23. Ciro Conversano, Alessandro Rotondo et al., 'Optimism and Its Impact on Mental and Physical Well-Being', *Clinical Practice & Epidemiology in Mental Health*, 6.1 (2010): 25–9.

24. Martin E. P. Seligman, *Learned Optimism: How to Change Your Mind and Your Life* (New York: Vintage, 2006).

But how do you capture that spirit? Where do optimism and hope come from when our brains so often seem disinclined to let us feel them? The way to understand the delicate interplay is to look at Spock from *Star Trek*, and Homer from *The Simpsons*.

Are we rational, analytical, Spock-like beings, obsessed with the logical assessment of probabilities for good or bad future outcomes based on available evidence? Or are we emotional Homers, feeling passionate hope or abject fear in great waves, for no real reason? This is a question a lot of philosophers and scientists have tried to answer over the years, because sometimes we human beings act a lot like Spock and sometimes a lot like Homer.

And the answer is that we are both:

Your Spock brain	**Your Homer brain**
Logical, analytical, thinking	Emotional, intuitive, feeling
Thinks in symbols, words and numbers	Feels in images, senses and stories
Needs to be taught, to have information, and never responds without thought	Responds automatically and in reaction to experiences
Slow	Fast
Dieting	Bingeing
Balancing a budget, planning a journey, reading an instruction manual	Smiling at a child, being scared watching a horror movie, dancing
Left part of your brain	Right part of your brain
Hard work	Effortless

A lot of the talk about climate change has been targeted towards the Spock brain – and it can unintentionally result in bucket-loads of pessimism. The focus on Spock thinking is natural because it's scientists who have worked out what is going on in the first place, and they are wary of emotional thinking and language because it's not a great mindset when trying to analyse complicated climate data. I'd want Spock as my brain surgeon, my accountant or my climate scientist. But Homer knows how to feel in reaction to Spock's conclusions – and often in unintended ways. Homer is also a lot more powerful than Spock when it comes to influencing our behaviour. We save up our 'Spock-ability' for big decisions, and let the 'Homer response' take care of almost everything else.

Which is probably why the scientists are getting so desperate. They are trying to talk to our inner Spocks, but ignoring their impact on an increasingly panicky Homer. Test it. There is a lot of climate science out there, so here's a short (but very important) bit of it:

> While there is low confidence in the detailed geographical projections of extratropical cyclone activity, there is medium confidence in a projected poleward shift of extra-tropical storm tracks. There is low confidence in projections of small spatial-scale phenomena such as tornadoes and hail because competing physical processes may affect future trends and because current climate models do not simulate such phenomena.

I have a postgraduate degree in this stuff. And if I drink a strong cup of coffee, sit down and really concentrate, then I can understand that paragraph. It's from the Intergovernmental Panel on Climate Change Report on how climate change can affect huge weather events like hurricanes. I read a lot of similar content before writing this book to be sure of my facts. But I can tell you that while it's desperately important, and fascinating in its own way, it's not fun. It's a Spock version of how Homer might say: 'Climate change is going to mean more big weather events, we just can't predict exactly where or when.' Although, to be honest, Homer would probably say: 'Wheeeee, big wind tunnel – let's ride it to Oz!'

We need to achieve some balance between our Spocks and Homers in order to remain optimistic. Spock wants facts and data; Homer wants images and emotions. And until now, most messages on climate change have been designed to inform Spock (and therefore terrify Homer). Most emotional or visual messages about climate change are even worse – so scary that our Homer brains often can't cope and just look away or think of something else. All this suppresses your optimism, leading to nasty pessimistic mindsets (bad for you and for the planet). So what's to be done?

There is one very quick fix. In one study, people who were asked to hold a pen in their mouth (causing them to inadvertently make the facial muscle movements characteristic of a smile) rated cartoons to be funnier than did other test subjects.

But another group of researchers tried to find a longer-term (and less embarrassing) way to trigger our inner Homer to feel good. They found that the most effective way to measurably increase optimism (with all the benefits that bestows) is to imagine a better future, in as much detail as you can and with yourself as the star of the show.[25] As they put it: 'Imagine yourself in the future, after everything has gone as well as it possibly could. You have worked hard and succeeded at accomplishing all the goals of your life...'

The exercise takes about 30 minutes to work through: fully imagining what your day might be like, where you would live, who you would see and be with, what you would be doing at each part of the day – eating, talking, working, travelling, etc. And for a happy hero the vision will include the wider world getting better too: what the lives of our family, friends, neighbours, colleagues, people on the street, on the TV and in other countries might be like. It's like your own personal version of John Lennon's 'Imagine'. But it shouldn't be too science-fictiony or unbelievable. No sky palaces of gold or alien overlords. As the researchers said, the vision should be of your life once you've worked hard and reached your goals.

This exercise makes Spock and Homer work together, so you neither panic nor get bored. Spock needs to think factually about what the outcome of your goals might be. And for a happy hero, Spock also needs to provide information about a cleaner, fairer and greener future – how our lifestyles and the world might change for the better. But it's Homer who must add colour and life to the picture. Homer feels the emotion and creativity of the vision. And if you get

25. J. M. Malouff and N. S. Schutte, 'Can Psychological Interventions Increase Optimism? A Meta-Analysis', *Journal of Positive Psychology* (2016): 1–11.

it right, you'll know the Homer part of your brain is working because you'll begin to feel uplifted and warm. You'll feel happier and excited. You'll feel enthusiastic and eager. You'll feel optimistic.

It's important to mention that the effects of this 30-minute exercise do fade over time. You'll need to keep exercising your optimism muscles in order for it to become your default mindset.

And your Spock brain might need a little help too – especially in the vision for a better world. So with that in mind, Chapter 7, 'A Good Life', provides you with a lot of detail about how great things will look and feel if we become happy heroes.

But just before we get to that you might want to grab a pencil to hold in your mouth, because we've finished the lessons now and you're about to be tested. There are some dangers to face before we get to the promised land.

Hold on to your hats – it's going to get choppy for a while…

*

The Story of a Happy Hero

'Are you feeling any dizziness?' the nurse asked gently.

'No, I'm fine thanks,' Jane answered, not quite looking her in the eye. She couldn't face her fully because then she might glimpse the needle and tube running out of her arm.

'Only a few more minutes,' her Aunty Em reassured her, looking totally at ease on the bed beside Jane. 'And if you want to speed things up, just squeeze your hand. Look, you can see the blood pumping out faster.'

'Thanks, Aunty Em, now I really am going to pass out,' Jane answered weakly.

Her aunt laughed. 'Nonsense, Janey. You've always been much stronger than you think. And you know, I'm pleased you finally came here with me.'

Jane had been meaning to donate blood for years. But as with most things, her good intentions had remained just that. Only when she, Chris and Ben had made a big wall chart of their plan had she finally added it to her list. And she was very much looking forward to ticking it off when she got home.

'I love coming here,' her aunt went on, looking around. 'It really restores your faith in humanity. I've met every type of person giving blood over the years, and it's always the same colour, whoever it's coming out of!' Aunty Em almost looked disappointed when the nurse came to remove the needle, although Jane was very grateful to be out of the donation room.

After a recovery tea and biscuit, Em hustled Jane outside and said, 'Right, what's next on your list? Shall we buy those bird boxes for your garden? Or the vegetarian cookbook you wanted?'

'Slow down, Em!' Jane interrupted. 'Let's just go sit in the park for a while. I'm still a bit shaky, to be honest.'

'Of course, dear.' Aunty Em looked amused. 'Would you like to take my arm?'

Jane just rolled her eyes. Her aunt seemed to have unlimited energy and was always trying to rope her into projects and activities

– although today Jane had been very grateful to have Em with her at the blood-donation centre, not least because as a regular donor, Aunty Em was a confident guide through the process.

The park was only a few minutes away, but when they arrived it wasn't quite the oasis of calm Jane had been hoping for. There seemed to be some sort of small demonstration going on. An earnest-looking young man with a beard and clipboard walked right up to them. 'Can we count on your support?' he asked, holding the clipboard out to them.

'Oooh, I love a good old-fashioned petition,' Aunty Em answered, looking around eagerly at the demo. 'Support for what?' she added.

'The new wind farm out to the west of town, beside that terrible golf course,' the young man explained. 'It got planning permission, but the MP here has said he'll block the turbines being built. He says they'll ruin the view. But we think he only cares about the golf course!'

'Right,' Aunty Em said, 'you just hand that petition over here. We'll sign it.'

'Actually, Em,' Jane objected, 'can we just go and sit down for a bit? I already feel like I've done my good deed for today.'

'I'll be with you in a minute, Janey.' Em was concentrating on the form. 'I want to hear more from this young man about the saga of the good turbines versus the dastardly MP.'

With a small sigh, Jane moved away from the crowd and found a quiet spot under a large oak tree. She took a deep breath and started to feel better almost immediately, with the sunlight dappling the leaves and the sound of birds still audible despite the traffic and crowd nearby.

When Aunty Em strode over, Jane asked her, 'Did you sign for me too? I do support it, I just needed a sit down.'

'Of course,' Aunty Em answered. 'I do love all these new renewable-energy thingies. I would have even added your dad's name too,' she went on, 'but that old sod's been a stick-in-the-mud since we were children and he doesn't approve of petitions or the like!'

'I don't know about that,' Jane said. 'He came over as a surprise yesterday with a water butt to catch the rainwater off our roof, to use on the garden rather than wasting water with the hose.'

'Golly,' Aunty Em laughed. 'We'll make an eco-warrior out of my dear brother yet!'

'Just don't mention the wind turbines,' Jane answered, 'or he'll start a petition in support of the golf course.'

Suddenly, Aunty Em looked a little mischievous. 'Perhaps,' she said, 'but he might just surprise you again one of these days.'

5

Being Tested

The absence of alternatives clears the mind marvellously.

—Henry Kissinger

Happy heroism isn't always easy. We all face challenges and you will likely experience many moments of doubt, now and in the future. You might feel very motivated for a while after reading this book, but then, as time passes, slip back into your old ways of thinking and acting. People might try to stop you, undermine you or tell you it's not worth it. And your own mind might even try to block you, especially as you start your Happy Hero Action Plan. So this chapter sets out what to watch for, how to dodge the most common pitfalls in the hero's journey and how to climb right back out if you fall into any of them.

I remember the exact moment when I gave up. All my agency, optimism and excitement about the future just drained away and a great sense of defeat swept over me. As the weight of despair pressed down, I felt like my heart stopped beating in my chest. I couldn't breathe for the sense of loss and hopelessness.

In that moment, I was standing in the middle of the Amazonian rainforest. I'd been there for hours, and the intense humidity had been sucking the breath out of me. The air tasted wet, and the trees, seemingly the height of skyscrapers but dripping with thick, sinuous vines, pressed in all around.

It had taken days of travel to get there, with special permissions needed along with safety briefings from experts. That morning I had boarded a tiny 10-seater plane to fly over the ocean of trees to a landing strip so deep in the forest I couldn't even see it until we were on it.

But I hadn't come to explore the mysteries and wildlife of the greatest rainforest on earth. I was wearing a hard hat, ear plugs and bright-orange safety jacket, and was standing on a concrete island carved out of the heart of the Amazonian jungle, because I'd been invited to visit an oil and gas extraction plant. The people working at the site were friendly and helpful, and very eager to welcome visitors to the high-tech rig that was pumping oil and gas out from underneath the rainforest itself. One of the customs of the place was to pour crude oil over the hands of newcomers as they arrived, and even hours later I could still smell the sharp tang of it on me.

Our tour had reached the gas-storage part of the plant (gas is often found along with oil). We were standing under the bulge of a huge white globular container, one of four 50-foot-tall gas-storage globes that stood surrounding a gas-flaring pipe. And as I watched the flame of excess gas flaring off from the top of the pipe over and above the tips of the trees, that's when the sense of defeat punched me. The fire almost seemed to be laughing at me. As it danced and spun I could hear it call out: 'It's too late! You can't fight me and you can't stop me. It's too late. It's too late.' The flame was hypnotic, and for one breath I believed it. I thought to myself that if human beings can build an oil rig in the centre of a rainforest, then who was I kidding? We chop down ancient forests, we pollute, waste, persecute and destroy. Nothing could undo what we've already done. It was too late, and all my work, all my hope, all my plans for the future were foolish and in vain. As I felt myself give up, my breath caught in my throat and my shoulders began to drop down, defeated.

Just then a siren screamed out. The people around me hesitated for a second, and then started to shout: 'Run… run!' The guide grabbed us and pointed to a bunker door at least 30 metres away. Disorientated in the heat and with sweat running into my eyes, I was the last to move. The guide shouted at me over the wailing siren: 'It's a fire!' And as we ran towards the bunker, in our ill-fitting orange safety jackets and hard hats, I spotted a curl of smoke rising from the tangle of pipes to one side of us. From feeling like it was about to stop just seconds before, my heart was now pounding so hard I could hear it as I gasped for breath in the heat. And in that moment, I realised I was stuck on top of a bomb, with thousands of barrels' worth of oil and gas all around and below me. If one spark reached all that fuel, then the plant I was on would become a huge crater blown out of the forest.

Then, as suddenly as it had started, the siren stopped. The brave people who had been holding open the bunker door and desperately herding us in slowly stood up and looked around. Our guide listened for a moment to his walkie-talkie and said: 'It's under control, nothing to worry about. Let's continue the tour.' But I didn't listen to much more. My mind was racing and my heart was still pounding as we walked around the rest of the plant. I was thinking about the flame and the bomb. And thinking about the people who had held open the door for me and the guide. Most of the group had been there by the entrance to the safety bunker, watching us anxiously, even though they themselves weren't safe yet. We had been a tour group for only one day and yet we acted like a community who cared about each other. And I thought about the flame, but rather than viewing it as a symbol of all that was wrong, I saw it as proof of human ingenuity. The oil and gas plant was an undeniably impressive human achievement: a sign of our engineering ability, our hard work and even our vision. But, like all our creations, temporary. In a few years, it could be as though this rig never existed. We have dismantled and remade whole cities before. We no longer watch as prisoners are fed to lions in the Coliseum, nor do we power our street lamps with hundreds of tonnes of whale oil. Humanity has proven its ability to grow and change, and to clean up the mistakes of the past.

As we prepared to leave the oil plant, I realised that just as we'd made that concrete island, we'd also made climate change. And as I looked over my shoulder I spotted the now tiny flame over the treetops and said: 'We made you, and we will unmake you. We have time.'

A few days later, I was lazily trailing my hand in the waters of the Amazon river. The boatman smiled and raised an eyebrow at my hand and said: 'Many things in the river might like that as a snack.' He laughed as I pulled my hand out and explained that he'd spent years ferrying tourists along the river to the spot where the deep-orange

Amazon river swirls into the black waters of the Rio Negro. While we watched these two rivers merge in an everlasting swirl of colour, he told me how every morning he takes the local children living by the river to school. Each one is learning to read and write (often the first in their family to do so), and part of their curriculum is about how to protect their forest and even how to fight climate change. He offers to ferry the kids in his boat for free, as he believes the future of his beloved river is in their hands. I smiled at him and said: 'It's in all of our hands.'

Facing Your Demons

Do you remember the crisis curve (see Chapter 1) with the monsters of denial and doom positioned to lead us along the path to disaster? Well, you got past the guards that time and continued your training. But now you're on the cusp of becoming a true happy hero, and that draws out the subtle tricksters and shapeshifters who will try to block you again. These new tempters will try to pull you away from the happy-hero path, but they have been very well studied and previous heroes have left advice on how to get past them.

The things psychologists struggle with most when they work with people facing crises are called 'maladaptations'. These are mind-sets that cause us crazy humans to wriggle around, make deals with or try to trick the great big crisis curves we face. And most of us will be confronted with some, or perhaps even all, of them in our journey, over and over again as we build better lives in a better world.

A blind maladaptation is a decision or behaviour that might seem reasonable at the time but can be harmful in the long term. It can mean trying to hang onto the status quo, even though you know you can't. It's a maladaptation to accept there is a problem, but think you don't have to do anything about it; or to make some changes, but stay too close to the behaviours that led you to the crisis curve in the first place.

It's quite fascinating looking at all the squirming we do and the avoidance tactics we use individually and collectively to try to avoid positive change – except that they are holding us back from an amazing future, which is a problem. You might have experienced many of the reactions yourself, so later on I've provided a general 'antidote' to help you recover from them. Good luck!

Blindness 1: The Excuse Machine

Do any of these sound familiar?

- It's too hard.
- It's too expensive.
- I'm too busy.
- It's too confusing.
- I don't know what would really make a difference.
- Others are much worse than me.
- I will do something eventually, but later.

Lots of us care about big problems like climate change, but we don't always do much about them. We all have a million excuses why we don't act, and we use them for eating unhealthily, wasting money, smoking and all the other things we feel guilty about but keep doing. Our incredible brains can generate convincing arguments against anything we don't want to do. And that's a big problem, because right now most of us don't want to change our behaviour to change the world. If we see taking positive action as just a chore, duty or hassle, then we'll only act because we feel guilty. And if guilt is our only motivator, then we've already lost the race. Instead of feeling guilty we should be searching for amazing solutions with built-in payback for the things we really want. And that will make our lives immeasurably better.

Blindness 2: Discounting the Future

This is one you might well be familiar with. We human beings often, and disastrously, 'discount' the future. Our desire for immediate gratification is far more influential over our behaviour than our long-term well-being. We'll eat cake today and promise ourselves to diet tomorrow. And if changing the world seems like a bore, then we'll leave all the requisite boring behaviours for our future selves to do, while telling ourselves that we don't have to change anything today.

Acting today for the benefit of the future can be hard. And it's tempting to assume that our future selves can make all the hard choices and perform the difficult actions we don't want to do today. Many beneficial behaviours, from exercise to saving for a pension, suffer from this 'I'll-do-it-tomorrow' syndrome. That's why in the early days of becoming a happy hero you have to pick the most fun, most fulfilling actions. After a while your brain will start to look forward to positive action, and that becomes a positive reinforcement.

Blindness 3: The Bystander Effect

I spend quite a lot of my time riding on the London Tube. Once, I was sitting there in the boredom coma most people experience on the Underground when a woman started to board the train with her baby. But just as she was getting on, one of the stroller wheels got caught in the gap between the platform and train. The doors suddenly started to close, but the stroller was still trapped against the outside of the train. As the mother desperately tore at the safety straps to try to free her baby, the buggy and child shuddered as the train began to move. In the carriage we all sat aghast, watching in horror. Then I jumped up and pulled the emergency alarm to stop the train. Thankfully, everyone was fine, and I was congratulated for 'quick thinking' by my fellow passengers and tearfully hugged by the baby's mother, which was nice, but not deserved. If I'd really been thinking quickly, I would have pulled the alarm the moment the stroller got stuck and before the doors even started closing. I wasn't fast; I was simply the first to overcome what's called the 'bystander effect' – probably because I knew it existed.

The psychological phenomenon of the bystander effect means that the more people know about a given problem, the less likely it is that one of them will take action. Trying to overcome your own bystander effect can sometimes be embarrassing, but it can also save lives. Since learning about it, I've become the person who asks, 'Is this anyone's bag?' at airports if I spot an unattended case. I'll ring the superintendent if the lift breaks down, rather than assuming someone else will. It's kind of annoying knowing that I can't simply offload responsibility now I know about the bystander effect. But in cases where it matters, like that day on the Tube, I've been grateful for that knowledge.

Climate change suffers from the biggest bystander effect ever. Everyone knows how serious it is, so we all assume someone else must be fixing it. And it's not just people but entire countries that suffer from this. How many times have you heard that there's no point in us taking action to halt global warming unless China (or India or the US) takes action first? That's being a bystander.

But now you know about it, it will be easier for you to be the person who raises the alarm, for problems big and small.

Blindness 4: The Righteous World

Would you have enjoyed *Die Hard* so much if Hans Gruber had outsmarted everyone and flown off with the loot, leaving John McClane behind as a patsy? Or if, at the last minute, Sauron had reached the Cracks of Doom and snatched the ring from Frodo before crushing and humiliating Gandalf and Aragorn in battle?

Probably not. From novelists to Hollywood scriptwriters, storytellers have always known the danger of failing to provide a satisfying ending. That doesn't mean all endings must be happy, but rewards and punishments need to be fairly handed out.

Every childhood story, every Hollywood movie and even religions teach that, eventually, rewards go to the good and punishments to the bad. This is called the 'righteous-world' mindset, and it runs very deep. Many of us believe that the world is basically orderly, stable and fair. Karma, Providence, divine justice and fairy-tale endings seem as solid and expected as 'what goes up must come down'.

The problem is that climate change can seem to violate that righteous-world belief. The impacts of climate change are arbitrary, and the innocent and poor are already suffering more than those who are causing the problem. When people who hold righteous-world beliefs are shown messages about climate-change disasters, their scepticism goes up because they simply can't accept that something so unfair, global and catastrophic could happen.[1] More people believe in righteous outcomes than you might think. I suspect that in my heart I do too, a little bit. I have too many fairy tales, happy-ending movies and parables in my subconscious. Rationally, I know the world doesn't work like that; bad things happen to innocent people. And I know that climate change is a chemical and physical process, rather than a moral judgement on those who cause it. But sometimes it can be too hard to align the reality of climate change with the stories in my heart.

Thankfully, there is one way in which just-world beliefs and reality do meet, and that's in the benefits of action. Acting on climate change really is good for the people who do it. Being good will be rewarded just as the righteous-world mindset says it should be. When people who trust in the righteous world hear about the benefits of taking positive action, they find it easier to accept climate change.[2] Although the arbitrariness of climate change doesn't fit their world-view, it is true that taking positive action on the climate is personally rewarded. So although the righteous theory doesn't work automatically, you can make it real through your climate-friendly actions. And the more you share the benefits you've felt by taking positive action with your friends, family and colleagues, the more you'll help the world to become truly righteous.

Blindness 5: Get Out of Jail Free?

Imagine sitting next to a heavy smoker at a bus stop. You can smell the smoke on them and see the nicotine stains on their fingers. With one hand they keep bringing their cigarette up to their lips and taking a drag from it, while every few seconds they cough violently and heavily into the other. You can hear them wheeze as they breathe.

They fumble in their pocket and drop something by your feet. To avoid another round of coughing, you swiftly reach down and sweep up what they've dropped to hand back to them. You notice it's a tube of cough drops. They thank you, and as they pop one into their mouth they complain to you: 'These cough drops don't really help.

1. M. Feinberg and R. Willer, 'Apocalypse Soon? Dire Messages Reduce Belief in Global Warming by Contradicting Just-World Beliefs', *Psychological Science* (US National Library of Medicine, 22 January 2011).
2. Ibid.

I've had this cough now for ages. I might complain to the company who make them – they haven't helped my chest at all.'

What would you think? Would you agree that the cough drops weren't working to solve the bad chest, or instead think that the smoker was in complete denial about their real problem?

The smoker's belief that their cough-drops are the problem (rather than the cigarettes) is the most common type of maladaptation, and it's called 'bargaining'. Bargaining is a symptom of facing a crossroads but desperately trying 'workarounds' in a doomed attempt to avoid real change. These bargains can be incredibly creative, and the lists of them go on and on – until people realise what they are doing and deal with the real issues they face.

An awful example of this bargaining applies to climate change, and it's called 'geo-engineering'. This is an innocuous term for huge potential experiments in our seas and skies. It is the cough sweet of climate change – bargains and avoidance tactics that let us keep burning fossil fuels while attempting to dampen down the consequences.

Geo-engineering plans have included proposals to dump a load of tiny mirrors into our atmosphere or create billions of 'microbubbles' in our oceans, both of which are intended to reflect the sun's rays away from the earth. Another idea was to 'fertilise' the world's oceans with tiny iron particles to promote the growth of carbon-gobbling algae. This is a great example of the unintended consequences of geo-engineering: a careful study[3] proved that adding iron would indeed allow big batches of algae to grow and reduce carbon, but the algae would be toxic to humans. The study explained how the poison would enter the food chain through fish before it had any impact on the climate.

Geo-engineering tries to avoid any real change, and instead uses technological interventions to try to cool down the planet once the worst kicks in. This approach means no payback from taking positive action, no massive improvements in our lives, just 'carry on' regardless and try to cope. Geo-engineering has been called 'a bad idea whose time has come' by journalists,[4] but the Royal Society in Lon-

3. J. G. Shepherd, Working Group on Geoengineering the Climate, 'Geoengineering the Climate: Science, Governance and Uncertainty', The Royal Society, 98pp.

don (Isaac Newton, Albert Einstein and Marie Curie were members) has a different idea. It reviewed all the evidence, research and experiments and concluded that the smartest geo-engineering choice is to stop it. We already have one planet-wide geo-engineering experiment under way: it's called global warming. Radically cut pollution, switch to renewable energy and plant a lot more trees instead is the Society's practical answer.

Geo-engineering is the kind of idea that pops up at crisis crossroads: a big, crazy and expensive way to try to avoid changing things for the better. Thankfully, most geo-engineering plans are swiftly shelved.

And as happy heroes we know these crazy plans aren't needed. Because we don't want either the cough drops nor the cigarettes. We want a happy, healthy and better life instead.

The Antidote

These are the five big ways in which our brains try to trick us out of being happy heroes, and we can all be tempted by them. Basically, anyone who is desperately promising that 'nothing really needs to change', or talking about problems like climate change as being far off and far away – is facing the future backwards. And that's a good way to bump into the crisis crossroads, but a crazy way to get out of it.

With a bit of happy heroism, however, you'll become a ninja of positive change. Because the only real way to change for good is to enjoy it. And enjoy it your way! Are there any actions in Chapter 4, 'Learning Heroism', that sounded like they would deliver a reward that you value? If you want an immediate antidote, then do one thing on your list right now and imagine all the rest of us as your cheerleaders, chanting your name and applauding you furiously. That's the way to cure any of these mindsets: take action to make a difference and enjoy it.

There are lots of other maladaptations that affect big groups

4. Deborah Zabarenko, 'Geo-Engineering: A Bad Idea Whose Time Has Come?' Thomson Reuters, 9 December 2011.

of people's response to climate change. Governments make big announcements about climate change but take little action. Companies realise 'green' is in, so they slap a 'Made with natural ingredients' label on their products, but change nothing about their manufacturing or shipping processes. People get tired of hearing that the climate is warming, and instead of doing anything about it they just tune out the message.

Our happy-hero philosophy is designed to avoid or vault over these barriers. Enjoy change and these problems will slowly slip away.

The Doubts

But even after you've dodged past the tricky maladaptations, you might still be plagued by doubts. In the next chapter I'm going to ask great things of you, so we need to make sure any misgivings are cleared up now.

Are any of the following still holding you back from happy heroism?

This All Sounds Great, but I Still Just Can't Get Motivated to Start

Beginnings are hard. Often we think we must 'start big' and change our lives overnight. But why not start with something tiny? Take a deep breath and think of something small you can do right now, either for the planet or for another person. It's got to be so small you can do it without any preparation or planning. Turn out an unnecessary light that's been left on? Switch off a plugged in appliance? Thank someone for having made you a tea earlier? Make someone a coffee? Pick up a piece of litter? Smile?

There. You've started! That's it – that's how easy this is. Next, try and do three more things today. And when you go to bed tonight, just before your eyes close, think about those things you did and congratulate yourself for making a start. Because every hero must start somewhere.

But It's Not Really 'Doing Good' if You Expect a Reward!

That's an argument that's been raging on since Plato. Is something really 'altruistic' or good if the person doing it hopes for a benefit in return? Neither philosophers nor biologists have been able to decide on an answer yet. So I'll just say that this book deals with impacts rather than intentions. A good impact still feels good whether the person who did it was sacrificing themselves or hoping for a reward. The climate doesn't care why we save it, nor do the people already suffering. If you donate blood, the person whose life that blood saves will be grateful that you did so – they won't care why.

But I'm So Small, and All of This Is So Big!

You are a superhero. Maybe you don't have the fluttering cape or abs of steel yet, but by reading this book you've proven yourself to be someone who matters. That makes you a hero in my eyes. Changing your mindset and helping to inspire others might not sound huge, but it's the most influential thing any human being can do. And I promise you: it will save the world.

Still feeling small? Well, together we are big, and we need you. Come and find us other happy heroes. Find the millions of us. We need you to encourage us when *we're* feeling small. We need you to share your successes and struggles. We need to know that *you're* making a difference because it motivates *us*.

And look after yourself. Eat healthily and take some exercise. Floss. Sleep. Take out insurance. Look both ways when crossing the street. Treat yourself the way a top coach treats a star athlete: push yourself towards your goal but take care of yourself along the way. You're worth it. And we need you.

But Climate Change Is Terrifying

True. But the future can be wonderful.

Worrying is exhausting. And remember that worrying isn't the same as doing. All the worry and doubt can turn into procrastination.

Anxiety kills action. So dump the worry and fear, and hold onto your vision of our amazing future with both hands.

The very best, in fact the only, antidote to fear is action. Get up right now and do something. Do something from your action list you haven't done before. Do something bigger than usual.

Feel the power. Climate change doesn't stand a chance against us.

But the Deniers Are Attacking Me

I've received nasty emails, trolling and even hate mail. I've even been called 'the climate sceptics' crumpet'!

I've had it all, and it makes me feel horrible. The desire to hit back or to just keep quiet and avoid confrontation is strong. But remember, there is a big difference between the professional deniers (who have a vested interest) and normal folk who are scared, threatened by or sceptical of climate change. The online trolls who attack people trying to make a difference are more tricky. They are trying to shut you up and protect their power. Fight back by rereading your list of actions, hanging out with some lovely happy heroes and then being louder, prouder and even more effective than ever – all with a big smile. That's what I do. And it works.

But the Doom Monsters Are Attacking Me

It's weird that environmentalists can get so angry at people who are also trying to save the world but having fun while doing it. The advice for tackling deniers and doomers is the same: stay strong and save 'em anyway.

But No One Else Really Cares!

I do.

Everyone else reading this book does.

The millions of people worldwide who are members of community groups, vote green and perform happy-hero behaviours all care.

We're all here. We're with you. Maybe it isn't obvious in your family, school, workplace, among your friends or community right now, but trust me, we are out here. Come find us.

But I Feel Ridiculous Calling Myself a 'Happy Hero'

No problem. You can be a change-maker, patriot, tree-hugger, good person, visionary or superhero. Or you can just be you.

The happy-hero label helps us to find each other, but it's just a label. You can do everything in this book and make a real difference without wearing the happy-hero T-shirt!

The mindset is what matters.

But I'm Really Angry about [Insert Cause of Anger Here]

It's hard to be positive about the future when you're so angry about the present. Every day a politician, company or even neighbour does something that rattles us. Remember, being a happy hero doesn't mean happily sitting back and waiting for things to be fixed. Being a happy hero doesn't mean quietly asking for permission. The thing you're angry about is probably a maladaptation or a denial/doom monster.

You've got a choice. Angry about coal pollution? Become a community wind-farm campaigner. Angry about deforestation in the Amazon? Go veggie and convince everyone you know to buy Forest Stewardship Certified wood.

Don't like something bad? Make the good a better alternative.

But We're All Doomed Anyway, Right?

Nope. And you need to read the next chapter immediately.

But the Climate Science Is Too Complicated

Climate science is supposed to be complicated. The climate is complicated. Thankfully, there are loads of books, websites, online talks and even cartoons that explain it all clearly, without anyone needing a doctorate to understand them. Visit the happy-hero website for a list of good examples.

But the Stuff You Recommend Is Too Expensive

I'm recommending a new mindset. Some of the exciting things in this book are beyond everyone's reach right now. Others, like talking to your neighbours, should be possible whoever and wherever you are.

Being a happy hero isn't dependent on income, but on motivation.

But You Fly a Lot – What Right Do You Have to Talk about Climate Change?

This is a hard one, because flying sucks. It exhausts human beings, empties their wallets and fills the sky with carbon. I would prefer a train, a bus or even a pogo stick to a nine-hour red-eye flight.

But I do take flights. In fact, I probably fly more than most people reading this, all in the name of saving the world, and the irony of that isn't lost on me. For years, I've been meeting business and government leaders all over the world to convince them to invest in carbon reduction. And I've been pretty good at getting major commitments out of them.

Flying isn't glamorous. I hate it. But living, breathing human beings meeting each other is the best way I've ever found to make change. There's the rub. It's visceral and intangible, but my ability to inspire, cajole, charm and bully works far better in person than in virtual space. I live with the irony and will be at the front of the queue if someone invents a better way.

My life otherwise is car-free, meat-free and renewable-powered. I hope happy heroes think my travel is worth it.

But Being Green Is Boring

Being a superhero isn't boring. It's challenging, tiring, scary sometimes and awesome. If you want to have more fun, then try some of the suggestions in Lesson Three: Have Fun section of Chapter 4.

My Partner/Boss/Best Friend/Brother-In-Law Says This Is Stupid

That happens a lot. It's hard when the people you're closest to don't get it. Remember that you're not a preacher, you're not angry and you aren't going to drown them in facts.

It's best to just get on with becoming a happy hero yourself. Change your own lifestyle and talk about how great you feel. No one wants to be argued into being good, but being inspired into it can be a pleasure.

But We Need to Do It All RIGHT NOW!

Chill. As Bill Gates says: 'Most people overestimate what they can do in one year and underestimate what they can do in ten years.' *You* get started, stay motivated and draw more people in. Then just watch what happens once you're with us.

Isn't Everything Just Going to Get Worse?

It can be hard holding onto your optimistic mindset after spending a few minutes looking at the world around you. It causes 'FUD' – Fear, Uncertainty and Doubt. The thing is, things aren't actually getting worse (although that might come as a surprise). And they might be about to get a LOT better.

Let me tell you how…

*

The Story of a Happy Hero

Everything was perfect.

The clothes rails and hangers were set up in corners of the living room. Jane had put out drinks and nibbles on side tables, and Chris had carried down her full-length mirror to lean against the window. She'd even printed off the 'Rules of the Rail' and pinned them up. Everything was ready for her first Swishing party.

As she tied little tags around hangers, Jane ran through, again, the list of who might turn up. Aisha seemed to know everyone in the office, even people from different departments. Jane knew the invitation they had sent out together by heart now, having spent a few sleepless nights trying to write the perfect one:

You are invited to a Swishing Party!

Bring any clothes, shoes or jewellery that you love but don't wear anymore.

And perhaps discover a new look for yourself.

(Please bring at least one good-quality used item, and more if you can!)

Jane had even included a careful map showing a shortcut to her house with the invite. Aisha was enthusiastic because lots of women in the office had mentioned they might come along. But as 5.30pm got closer, Jane began to worry. If only a few people turned up, then there wouldn't be enough clothes to make the event exciting. And it would be really obvious that she'd been expecting more people because of all the glasses and drinks she'd put out. Jane realised she was just standing watching the clock and worrying. So she went into the kitchen for a quick cup of tea. And to log onto the parenting website.

She had been posting all the things she and Ben had been doing, and the mysterious Godmother had been encouraging her. But others had now started to join in too. In fact, the thread she'd originally commented on about climate change was becoming quite popular. The Godmother was no longer the only person making suggestions. Jane was scanning through all the posts with a smile when an appointment reminder suddenly popped up on her screen: '5.30pm – Swishing Party!'

She hadn't realised it was already time. She got up quickly, smoothed down her skirt and went into her front room to wait for the first knock... And she stood there... Then she went to sit on the edge of the sofa... After 10 minutes she pulled out her phone and texted Aisha: 'Are you on your way?' She'd actually been expecting her best friend to arrive early. But Aisha wasn't here. No one was here. Her chest started to feel tight and she realised she was biting the edge off a nail. Was this really happening? Was no one coming?

By 5.50pm she felt like a total fool, sitting alone in a room set up for a party. How was she going to explain to Chris and Ben that no one had bothered to turn up, not even Aisha? She slumped down in a chair as her eyes began to fill.

When there was a knock at the door, it took her a moment to realise what it was. Waiting outside was a smiling group of women she vaguely recognised from the Accounts department. The chirpy lady at the front gave her a big grin and said: 'Sorry to be early, but we absolutely whizzed here! We've got oodles of stuff and thought we could help you set up.'

Jane must have looked a bit lost because the woman gushed on: 'Your directions were so fabulous we actually beat the time on Google Maps.' She laughed and held up a bag of clothes as if it were a magic password to get in.

'Sorry, of course,' Jane said, quickly gathering herself. 'Please, come in. You can start putting things up on the rail. I've attached little tags in case you want to write your name so people know who the clothes are from.'

The women bustled in and were a chatty, friendly lot. Even with just a few people the room started to feel busy. And over the next fifteen minutes more women turned up with bags of jewellery, clothes and shoes. Jane ran around helping them to find hangers and set out the earrings and necklaces on side tables, silently laughing at herself for forgetting she'd put 5.30pm in her diary rather than the actual start time of 6pm, to give herself time to prepare.

When there was another knock at the door, Jane opened it to

find a smiling but unusually nervous Aisha. Jane could understand why, because the CEO was standing right behind her. She welcomed them both in, dying to ask Aisha what was going on, but too polite to blurt it out.

The Swishing party was really under way by now, with women holding outfits up against themselves in the mirror and picking out pieces their friends might look great in. Jane herself hadn't really looked at the clothes because she was so busy welcoming, explaining and putting out extra drinks. But then Aisha came over, holding a gorgeous deep-green satin dress. It was tight-fitting and a size smaller than Jane usually wore. 'Try this on, Jane, it's a designer label!'

'It will never fit me,' Jane said, trying to shoo Aisha away. 'And anyway, where would I ever wear it?'

'It really would suit you,' the CEO said, having just wandered over. 'It's mine, actually. My assistant saw the Swishing party invite, and I thought I'd pop in too. You don't mind, do you?'

'No, no, it's lovely that you came – and brought something too,' Jane swiftly assured her, grabbing the green dress. 'I'll try this on upstairs.'

Jane had taken the dress mainly to avoid seeming rude to the CEO. But when she ran up to the bedroom and tried it on, she was surprised. The dress really did fit, and was the most glamourous thing she'd ever worn. Feeling bold all of a sudden, and wanting to show her appreciation, she wore the dress downstairs. 'Wow, that looks amazing!' said the bubbly lady who had arrived first, and the whole room stopped what they were doing for a moment to agree.

The CEO was smiling and said, 'I'm so pleased that dress is going to a good home.'

'Well, all the cycling must be paying off,' Jane answered with a laugh. 'I never thought I'd fit into it!'

The CEO looked thoughtful for a moment. 'Yes, that cycle-loan scheme was a very good idea.' She seemed to make a decision. 'Pop by my office tomorrow. I'd like to run a few other ideas past you.'

Jane wasn't sure how well a blush would match her new dress, so she politely agreed and bustled off to put out more nuts.

6

Find the Secret

To live now as we think human beings should live… is itself a marvellous victory.

—Howard Zinn

Let me ask you five simple questions about the world:

In the past 20 years, has the worst global poverty:

1. doubled
2. remained the same
3. fallen by half?

Compared to the 1990s, has violent crime in the US:

1. increased threefold
2. remained the same
3. dropped threefold?

In countries with the lowest equality for women (e.g. Qatar or Jordan), how do girls and boys perform at school by the age of 15?

1. Boys get better grades in everything (reading, maths, science).
2. Boys get better grades in maths and girls in reading.
3. Girls get better grades in everything (reading, maths, science).

In the poorest 30 countries in the world, are birth rates per woman:

1. five children or higher
2. average of four children
3. three children or lower?

Since 1955, have worldwide IQ scores:

1. lowered by more than 10 points
2. remained the same
3. risen by more than 10 points?

The correct answer to each one of the above questions is 3.

Are you surprised?

I would be surprised if you weren't surprised, because surveys reveal that most of us – over 70 per cent of Britons – think the world is getting worse rather than better. (When asked the question about global poverty falling or rising, only 5 per cent of Americans answered correctly that we're solving it.)[1]

Pessimism about the world around us and the direction we're taking seems to have become the norm. But as a happy hero you know how important hope is. And one of your hardest jobs is to accept that things have improved, and to believe they can get even better. We've read in previous chapters about the importance of optimism and how the Thomas Theorem subtly but strongly influences us to get what we expect. So an important part of my formula is that we must hold a positive vision of the future in our minds, and expecting and believing that things can get better is so much easier if you accept that they already have. Humanity has proven that it is able, in every generation, to right wrongs and make the world a better place for those to come. Each of us is living proof of how well this has been done and how much progress there has been.

This chapter is designed to help you believe that things can get even better, not as some sort of 'wishful thinking' but because of hard evidence. In fact, the positive trends are easy to find, if you know how to look for them:

1. Johan Norberg, *Progress: Ten Reasons to Look Forward to the Future* (London: Oneworld, 2016).

- **We're solving the worst types of poverty.** Back in 1820, well over 90 per cent of people across the world lived on less than $2 a day (in modern money). That's the official definition of 'extreme poverty', because at that level survival itself is in question. So it's only 200 years ago that most of humanity was living at subsistence level or below. But by 2015, less than 10 per cent of people were still surviving on that extreme low income, and we had halved it to that level only in the past 20 years. Which means that in your lifetime, poverty has fallen at its fastest rate in history. Humanity continues to face great challenges, from rampant inequality to helping those who are still incredibly poor, even if their poverty doesn't count as extreme. But I hold great hope that we can solve those problems, because we have already done more than any previous generation in raising living standards for everyone. It's the most amazing achievement, and yet so few people even know it's happening.
- **We're becoming less violent.** This one is even more surprising. Despite the daily horrors we see broadcast, between the 1990s and today the number of conflicts in the world fell by 40 per cent. And it's not only war and conflict that are falling, but all violence, and it's been falling for a long time. Today the average homicide rate globally is around eight people per 100,000 per year. By comparison, in 13th-century Europe it's conservatively estimated there were up to 80 murders annually per 100,000 people. If plotted on a graph, the decline over time looks like a slightly bumpy slide downwards. To a European from the Middle Ages, our society would seem astonishingly safe and civilised. Even our language and culture reflect this change towards peacefulness. A study by the Bristol Royal Hospital for Children in 2004 found that traditional children's nursery rhymes included 10 times more graphic violence than television programmes aired in Britain before 9pm. If you've never read the original *Grimms' Fairy Tales*, then take a look – but don't read them to your children!
- **We're better educated.** Literacy and numeracy have been on an upward curve globally for generations. But in the last few decades there has been an incredible jump. In the year I was born, 1974, only around half the people in the world

could read, but since then that number has grown, and now nearly 90 per cent are literate.[2] The huge effort by teachers, governments and students themselves means billions more people are now able to read a medicine bottle, newspaper or voting slip. And using international data, researchers at the University of Missouri and the University of Glasgow have determined that girls outperform boys in educational achievement in 70 per cent of the countries they studied, regardless of the level of political, economic or social equality in their countries. Education has been fighting a war against ignorance and exclusion, and winning.

- **Our population will stabilise.** There's no arguing that the growth in human population has been explosive. It has near doubled in my lifetime alone, putting a great strain on nature's resources. And it will continue to climb steadily, according to forecasters, reaching over 11 billion people by 2100. That's going to be hard to manage. But there is more to the population story than the overall number, because the actual global birth rate has been falling since the 1970s. Our population isn't growing because we're having more babies than ever before (in fact, average births per woman have dropped nearly everywhere), but because more of our children survive and we're all living longer. It will take time for our population to level out, as life expectancy keeps rising, but it will happen. And the good news is that healthy, educated, long-living adults have a fair chance of finding solutions to the world's problems.
- **We're smarter.** This one is my biggest surprise! Across the world our IQs are rising, especially in those places where health and educational attainment are good.[3] Political scientist Dr James Flynn, of the University of Otago in New Zealand, first discovered these IQ gains nearly 30 years ago. He found that a review of historical data reveals that over the past 100 years, Americans' mean IQ has been on a slow but steady climb. Between 1900 and 2012, it rose

2. Peter H. Diamandis, *Abundance: The Future Is Better Than You Think* (New York: Simon & Schuster, 2015).

3. James R. Flynn, *Are We Getting Smarter? Rising IQ in the Twenty-First Century* (Cambridge: Cambridge University Press, 2012).

> nearly 30 points, which means that the average American today has a higher IQ than 95 per cent of the population had in 1900. We now have this data for about 30 more countries, and it seems our global average IQ is increasing around six points a decade. This insight, above all, makes me hopeful for our children's (smarter) future.

And speaking of children, things have particularly improved for the youngest and most vulnerable in our societies. In the last 16 years, the number of children under 14 who are working (often in mines or sweatshops) has fallen by more than 50 per cent. And in the last 25 years, the mortality rate for under-fives has also dropped by 50 per cent. Add in rising educational standards and today, across the world, a child has a better chance of surviving and going to school than at any other time in history.

Most of these positive statistics and stories come from fantastic books and articles by the researchers Steven Pinker and Peter Diamandis. They are carefully measuring how we are making the world better, step by step. And they have many more examples besides those I've included here, from worldwide drops in HIV/AIDS infection, to the doubling of female politicians in the last 20 years.

Their work is hugely encouraging and proves that humanity can make great leaps in building better lives for everyone. But as you read all those positives you might well be asking: So, why doesn't it feel like things are getting better? In fact, why does it feel like they are getting worse?

If It Bleeds, It Leads

'If it bleeds, it leads' is the unspoken mantra of every newsroom. Ever since the first newspapers, followed by television entering our homes and now the internet, the media has always known that sensationalism sells. Competition for our attention has never been greater, with ratings and huge advertising revenue as the prize, and what draws us in is horror, anger and fear. Bad news far outweighs good, with as many as 17 negative news reports to every one that is positive. And a study by the Pew Research Center for People and the Press found that war and terrorism have consistently ranked as the stories we follow most closely since 1986, when the study began, with bad-weather and disaster stories not far behind.

The news conglomerates know all this very well. They use sophisticated 'media logic' algorithms to exploit it, tweaking the rhythm, grammar and presentation of news stories to elicit the greatest impact (and number of clicks), while the paparazzi will vie for the most brutal or heartrending image to shock you into paying attention. Because news is a money-making industry.

The result is that watching the news today can be psychologically risky. Being glued to your television, reading the paper or surfing the latest crisis online increases ratings and market share for the media companies, but it also raises the probability of your own pessimism and even the likelihood of depression. The world might be becoming safer and kinder in many ways, but our news is going the other way. And whereas in previous generations the (many more) horrors in the world might take days or weeks to be reported, and then just written up in long prose with no pictures, today you can watch horrors unfolding 'live'. Someone who has never been physically attacked, never experienced war, never gone hungry has seen thousands of high-resolution images of all those things. We know more, and in full-colour detail, about crises across the world than our forebears knew about the wars on their own doorsteps. And so although our own lives might be peaceful and safe, we end up believing we are beset by terrible threats.

Mindset Reset

The fear and horror messages matter. A whopping 81 per cent of Donald Trump's supporters think life has worsened in the past 50 years. Among Britons who voted to leave the European Union, 61 per cent believe that most children will be worse off than their parents. The tidal wave of fear and threat that floods across our screens affects our perception of the world, makes us depressed and unhealthy, and influences the way we vote and treat others. And it's been going on your whole life.

How can you retrain yourself to see the world as it truly is, both the good and the bad? One simple way to help reframe this for yourself is to think back through time. We all know that our lives today are healthier, freer and longer than those of peasants in medieval Europe. Back then the worst poverty meant death, only the aristocracy could read, women had few rights, and life expectancy was short thanks to plagues, child mortality and near constant war. Jump forward 500 years to the early 19th century, and child mortality and literacy levels in Europe weren't much better and the horrors of the global slave trade were at their peak, with millions of lives being stolen and people being enslaved and shipped as chattel across the world. Move further forward still, to the Great Depression of the 1930s, and nearly a quarter of Americans were unemployed (today's rate hovers at around 5 per cent) and almost half the children in the world didn't have enough to eat. Even the Swinging Sixties didn't swing for everyone: war raged in South America and Asia; in the US it was still illegal for black and white people to marry each other until late in that decade; and the cold war was starting to seriously heat up.

But in each of these eras, things were a bit better than they had been before, not only in Europe or North America, but across the world. Each generation has inched forward a little. If you're a woman reading this book in a country where you can vote, read and own property and have a low risk of dying in childbirth, then you are living a safer and more liberated life than most woman throughout human history. And it's conceivable that every other woman and girl could join you.

Thousands of 'yes, but' examples will be crowding your brain right now, and I agree we have no right to feel smug. Most of the progress I've outlined was made by those who came before us, people who fought against injustice, developed science and technology, resisted oppressive regimes and took action on behalf of others. Many died so that we could live the safer lives we enjoy now.

And if you're still struggling to believe the world can be better, then the next time horror happens, near or far from you, remember this quote from the children's entertainer Fred Rogers:

When I was a boy and I would see scary things in the news, my mother would say to me: 'Look for the helpers. You will always find people who are helping.'

I have looked. And in every tragedy, attack or disaster, it's true: there are always happy heroes helping.

Change Everything

Our job's not nearly done. The world might be better than you expected, but there is still suffering. We continue to face injustice and terror, and too many of our fellow humans are living without the benefits of progress. Just today you've probably read about yet another atrocity or outrage somewhere in the wider world (or closer to home). And while many of us may be safer and healthier than ever before, we're still beset by stress, worry and disease. And then there are all the new challenges that have emerged – notably climate change and the growing crisis in the environment. I'm asking you to accept how far we've come, but I'm not suggesting you kick back or decide the job's done.

None of the improvements throughout history came automatically. They happened because people like you decided to make the world a better place. We stand on the shoulders of past happy heroes, people who were prepared to make a difference.

Thomas Barnardo, the founder of the famous homes for poor children, originally wanted to become a doctor and a missionary to China. But when he arrived in London from Dublin in the early 19th century, alleviating the pitiful state of the children he found there became his life's work. At the time, Victorians thought poverty was a sign of sheer laziness or poor breeding, but Dr Barnardo couldn't bring himself to think that way about the children sleeping in gutters and on rooftops across the city. So he started to set up homes to house, feed and teach basic skills to street children, making a commitment that no child in need would ever be turned away. By the time he died in 1905, the charity Barnardo founded was running 96 homes that cared for more than 8,500 children. He was an extraordinary man, but he didn't change those Victorian attitudes on his own: other people helped to fundraise for the children's homes, stopped hiring child chimney sweeps, petitioned the government over children's rights and spoke to their neighbours about Barnardo's work. Hundreds and thousands of people helped the charity in large and small ways. And they didn't just save individual kids: together they encouraged an entire society to feel compassion for and protect children.

Today we can't imagine it being any other way. And now *you* are one of those hundreds and thousands. You need to believe that tomorrow can be better than today. No matter the horrors pumped out by the news or the great threats of things like climate change, your belief in the future will be the deciding factor in the future we actually get.

And you have backup, because there is a very special change already happening in the world, and it will amplify every positive action that you take. This magical element is already out there, but it's invisible most of the time. It's your secret weapon, your golden bullet, and the biggest factor in supporting you as you make changes in your own life and the world around you. And it's got your back as you work through your Happy Hero Action Plan.

Energy Is Everything

For every other animal species on this planet, there is only one thing that fuels everything they do: food. That's it. Eating is the basic transfer of energy from food to blood and muscle. Food keeps animals warm, allows them to move around, helps them to recover from illness or injury. Food keeps them alive.

But we human beings are a little different. We eat food for the basics like movement and growth, but we use a lot of 'outsourced energy' to do everything else. We burn coal to generate electricity and keep us warm, we burn oil to move our cars and planes around, and we use outsourced power for all the technology that fixes our injuries, powers our playthings and keeps our homes humming.

It's no surprise that as the world has become safer, more educated and healthier, our global energy consumption has boomed. Electricity, gas and petrol have powered the industries and inventions that have raised living standards. In the past a huge percentage of the world's population worked in the fields just to feed the rest, but since the Industrial Revolution machines have taken over a lot of dangerous, dirty or dull work, freeing more and more of us to be educated, entertained and to live longer. But all of those machines eat a lot of energy, and if we want to make the world a better place, we're going to need even more of it. We actually need terawatts of energy, each one being the equivalent of a lightning bolt (a million million watts).

The total power used by all us humans worldwide currently runs at only 16 terawatts per year. That's it. The energy we use, from oil to coal, gas, nuclear and even wood fires, is equivalent to just 16 lightning strikes a year. Doesn't sound like much, does it? Except it is. And while what we've achieved with all this outsourced energy is impressive on the one hand, it is also a little sad, because half of humanity still burns wood or animal waste to stay warm. And it's dark at night for them. With just a few more terawatts we could power every human's home, we could free people from machine-like work, we could fuel education, development and progress. Imagine what we could do with double what we have now, or imagine if we had 100 lightning strikes to play with, rather than just 16?

But there's a problem. The catch is that our current sources of energy simply can't provide more than we currently use. They are too rare, too expensive and too dirty. We must dig deeper for oil, crack open mountains to get at the coal and risk meltdowns for nuclear power just to keep up with what we already use. And even with all that effort, we might have less energy available as the fossil fuels get used up. Plus, of course, all the progress and freedom facilitated by those fossil fuels have also come at a cost: climate change. Energy is the secret to making the world a safer, smarter and more equal place, but we need more of it – and without all the nasty side effects of climate change, pollution or toxic nuclear waste.

Is there a smarter option?

We need to look for better, cleaner and cheaper options – something, thankfully, that geeks and entrepreneurs have been beavering away at for decades. *This* is the secret weapon which we happy heroes have backing us up. New forms of energy are going to transform the world around us for the better. You are living through this massive change. And this huge global energy shift is what I believe will make a better world possible, rather than us just wishing for one. So now let's take a sneaky peak at the huge energy revolution we're going to experience...

Antimatter

This is the super-freaky, wild and intense end of the energy spectrum.

Most self-respecting starships in science-fiction stories use antimatter as fuel for good reason: it's the most potent fuel known. And getting to the stars is simply beyond fossil fuels. The Starship *Enterprise* doesn't run on petrol, and the *Millennium Falcon* doesn't have a coal chute. While tonnes and tonnes of chemical fuel would be needed to propel a human mission to Mars, just tens of milligrams of antimatter would do it.

Here's the idea. If you read Dan Brown's *Angels and Demons*, then you might remember that when equal amounts of matter and antimatter meet, they annihilate each other. That massive reaction is so intense that it creates the highest energy density of any known propellant, making it possibly the most efficient energy source in the universe. How efficient? Well, the amount of antimatter fuel needed for a trip to Mars would be smaller than a pea. You could hold it in a teaspoon. And NASA is planning to use exactly that (eventually), because we can produce this stuff now. We're already making *Star Trek* fuel. At CERN, the huge particle physics lab in Switzerland, they are making tiny amounts of real antimatter. They even manage to keep it stable for a few hours. We can make it, but with today's technology it would cost about $100 billion to make enough to go to Mars.

Some of it also gives off nasty gamma rays, but the CERN scientists are starting to improve the formula to create cheaper (and less radioactive) antimatter. They've even developed carry cases for these tiny drops of terawatts, for when we've fixed the cost and radiation issues.

So your grandkids' personal spaceship could well be antimatter-fuelled, if we fund, research and decide we want it.

Nuclear Fusion

Energy holds together every single atom. It's what stops all the sub-atomic particles inside from flying apart. Split an atom and a tremendous amount of that energy is released as heat and light. This is called a fission reaction. That heat can be used to boil water, and the steam can turn turbines and generate electricity. And that's how today's nuclear energy works. The catch is that the split atom is then waste – nasty radioactive waste (exactly the stuff that got me into all this to begin with).

But fission has a good twin, called fusion. Instead of cracking atoms open, like in fission, fusion mates them up. Fusion power uses helium gas rather than uranium or plutonium – much less likely to spark a world war. Fusion works by pushing atoms into each other, hard, until they combine. But it's a forced marriage, so the squished atoms aren't stable and soon jump apart. Unlike the aggressive split of fission, this is more of a pop, and it releases only heat and helium, not broken radioactive atoms. Fusion is a lovely idea, and is already working in labs across the world.

It's the heat we want – to boil the water and turn the turbines. Basically, nuclear energy – be it fission or fusion – is a high-tech steam engine.

Visit the Culham Centre for Fusion Energy, in the rural English Oxfordshire countryside, and in an unimposing building you can see a nuclear-fusion chamber. It looks like the inside of a metal doughnut. The science works, but it's hard to reach a industrial scale and reasonable cost. No one has built a full-scale working fusion reactor, yet, but watch this space.

Earth Energy

Those first two energy sources are supercool, in a science-fiction type of way. As a happy hero it's helpful to know about the big positive breakthroughs which are coming. It helps bolster our hope and optimism. But the best news is already here, and it's started to change everything already.

We use the old fossil fuels of oil, gas and coal in the same way: we burn them. And as they burn, we move around, light things up, cook, do brain surgery and watch TV. Which is fabulous, except for two problems. Firstly, because things that burn up will ultimately run out, and there isn't enough for everyone. Coal, oil, gas and even uranium will run out, and we can't simply make more of them, so countries have a tendency to protect their resources with big guns. Secondly, fossil fuels don't just give off heat when we burn them; they also give off carbon dioxide, that sneaky, colourless, odourless gas that – as we know – wafts up to the atmosphere and traps too much heat on the planet.

So let's think about the planet, this unbelievably rich, watery, windy beauty we're travelling through the universe on at 67,000 miles per hour. Planet earth has already given us coal, oil and gas. But those are small fry compared to the earth itself. By using 'earth energy' we can harvest the waves, the wind and even the core heat just below the crust.

Welcome to grown-up energy. Welcome to planet-sized energy.

Wind, wave, tidal, geothermal and hydroelectric: these are all energy sources that harness the free power of our seas, the earth's crust, the weather and the water. This is energy from geography. According to the International Energy Agency, over 20 per cent of the world's electricity already comes from these renewables. Germany managed to supply all of its electricity needs from solar, wind, hydro and biomass plants during one Sunday in 2016, and energy costs went negative that day. Denmark beat that when their wind farms supplied 140 per cent of demand and they sold their energy surplus to neighbouring countries.[4] China's new target for renewable-energy generation dwarfs even Germany's, with gigawatts from wind and solar coming online every year.

If we start pumping out new wind turbines with the same

4. Jess Shankleman, 'Germany Just Got Almost All of Its Power from Renewable Energy', Bloomberg.com, 16 May 2016.

urgency as the US had when producing tanks and bombers in the Second World War, we could generate 3 million megawatts of wind power by 2020[5] – that's enough to meet nearly half of the world's energy needs.

But maybe wind's not your thing? Then try digging down to the heat trapped just below your feet. The geothermal energy contained in the uppermost 6 miles of the earth's crust is 50,000 times[6] more powerful than all our oil and natural-gas resources combined. That's gobsmackingly huge. Almost all homes in Iceland are already powered by this geothermal energy – heat from the earth itself.

Sunshine

Alternatively, we could just use the free energy pumped out by the biggest power plant in the solar system.

Over 99.9 per cent of life on earth is already solar-powered. It's the ultimate renewable – the huge entropy event in the sky. Almost all our current dirty fossil-fuel energy is solar energy anyway, just at a few degrees of separation. Plants photosynthesise by basically eating sunlight. Animals then eat the plants. Eventually the plants and animals die. After millions of years of being pressurised under mountains of rock, all those ancient dead animals and plants turn into coal and oil. When you think about it, when we burn coal or oil we're burning really old sunlight. It's gone bad and is past its sell-by date, which might be why it gives off that nasty carbon dioxide. It's a crazy situation when you realise we've got massive amounts of the fresh stuff hitting the planet every single day.

Remember nuclear fusion – the clean version, when atoms are squeezed into each other, then pop apart and release heat and light? That's what is happening in the sky every single day, on a humongous scale. The sun is a massive hydrogen-fusion reactor that's been burning for over 4 billion years and sending all its energy down onto the planet for free. The plants worked it out early on: their leaves are solar panels.

The sun provides enough energy in one hour to supply the

5. Lester Brown, *Plan B 3.0* (Earth Policy Institute, 2007).

6. Union of Concerned Scientists, 'How Geothermal Energy Works', n.p., 22 December 2014.

world's energy needs for one year.[7] OK, that deserves to be said again. Say it out loud and remember it: enough sunlight hits the earth in *one hour* to supply all of humanity's energy needs for *one year*.

No wonder almost all the biomass on the planet – every tree, plant, flower, crop and the huge amounts of algae – uses solar power. All that green stuff is the basis of our food chain. Every animal (including us) relies on sunlight hitting those plants in order to eat. Yes, of course it's more complicated than that. There's water and nitrogen and phosphorus and even carbon, but sunlight is the magic extra ingredient. The sun itself is a free energy source over a million times bigger than our entire planet. This vast nuclear reactor has gone through billions of years of shakedown trials. No terrorist is going to blow it up, no government can switch it off, no one can stick a flag on it and charge you to use it.

So earth energy, especially solar, means you can be your own energy company. When we are powered mainly by renewable energy, the world, and your life, will look a lot different. You and your local community will control your energy rather than it being transmitted from miles away. And because solar panels are smaller and cheaper than a power station, they can reach the remotest parts of the world and light up African villages and Himalayan camps. With enough energy, available to everyone – to grow food, recycle waste, clean water and power progress – many of the worst horrors of disease, famine and poverty can be solved. It will be cheap, abundant, safe and fair. It is the only way to smash through the energy glass ceiling and top that 16 terawatt limit.

As you start changing the world for the better, remember that the planet has your back. And the sun is your superhero sidekick.

Better Everywhere

We need light in the darkness. When it comes to poverty, that's not just a metaphor. For too many people, once the sun sets, that's it. No light for homework, no light for family time, no light to talk by, discuss politics,

7. Oliver Morton, 'Solar Energy: A New Day Dawning? Silicon Valley Sunrise', *Nature*, n.p., 6 September 2006.

gossip, draw, play, visit neighbours, fix things, sew and mend, clean, read or simply watch the faces of your loved ones.

But for only $5 you can make the most straightforward of solar lamps. Leave it in the sun all day and you get three hours of light at night. Or for slightly more you've got a tiny solar panel that produces enough energy every day for a few hours' light and to run a radio and charge a mobile phone. And that can change everything. It's the key to unlocking education, to giving people control, connection and power over their lives. Energy gives access to information, and information is power.

In the Himalayan winter the temperature can drop to –40°C and people get just six hours of daylight a day. Dangerous kerosene lamps provide extra lighting, for those who can both afford and travel to buy them. Enter the Barefoot College. The college recruits people from the poorest villages to train as 'barefoot engineers'. Once trained, they trek up into the highest passes and across treacherous rope bridges to install and repair solar panels in villages dotted throughout the Himalayas. They trudge up those mountains to bring light, heat and hope. Today nearly 500 engineers serve over 700 villages with solar energy.

'I now look back at my childhood, when I always dreamt of doing something big for my society. My mother laughed at me. Now my family and even the village elders respect me,' says Ritma, a barefoot solar engineer and impressive happy hero.

As happy heroes we already know that our positive vision for the future must be for everyone. We take this step together or not at all. Get this right and no one is left behind. Imagine what we'll achieve with billions of happy heroes. All we need to do is get some basics right: enough food for everyone to eat and clean water to drink; light and heat for homes; online access; education and healthcare.

One of the hardest jobs for a happy hero is accepting the possibility of a world where an image of starving babies or a disease-ridden shanty town would seem weird and outdated. Won't it be extraordinary when that just doesn't happen any more?

That's what I'm asking of you.

To believe that is possible.

And then work to make it real.

*

The Story of a Happy Hero

Chris gave Jane a big hug. 'Don't be nervous, love,' he said. 'I'm sure she just wants to congratulate you on the cycle-scheme thing.'

'I don't know,' said Jane, clearly worried. 'It seemed to be about more than that. What if she asks me for another idea?'

'Then I guess you'll just have to come up with one,' Chris grinned down at her. 'You don't seem short of them around here! I've spent my weekend digging the garden for your vegetables.'

'Hey,' she said, gently pushing him away. 'The vegetable patch was your idea! And anyway, you and Ben spent more time playing with worms and building mud castles than digging!'

'Maybe you could suggest a company allotment to the CEO,' Chris teased, as he kissed her goodbye.

On her cycle into work Jane kept worrying about the upcoming meeting. Although she was proud of all the changes her family was making, she still didn't feel like an expert, especially when it came to what a whole company should do about climate change. By the time she reached the CEO's office, she was fervently wishing that Aisha had never raised her hand in the meeting, and even that the Godmother had never replied to her original post.

The CEO was welcoming but seemed a little distracted as she spoke to some other executives in her office. 'Come in, come in, Jane, take a seat.' She waved her to a spot at the table. 'Can someone pass Jane a copy of the climate plan?'

With a sinking feeling, Jane realised the meeting wasn't just between her and the CEO, but a wider group of people she'd never met, all gathered to discuss the company's climate goals.

She glanced down at the document and saw it was filled with jargon about 'CO2e', 'COP21' and 'Parts per million GHGs'. Jane's heart sank. Although she'd been helping Ben learn about climate change and making a difference in the world, most of it had been about the basics, and they'd gone off on tangents learning about solar cookers in Africa or how recycling works. She wasn't sure the kids' science websites they'd explored together would quite cut it in this room.

'Right, has everyone had a chance to glance through? Yes? Good,' the CEO started. 'This is just a preliminary meeting for feedback. There've been a few different contributors to the paper, so they can introduce their sections in turn and we'll take questions and ideas.'

An enthusiastic young woman with glasses started off, taking them through technical plans for energy efficiency in factories. It all sounded pretty comprehensive to Jane, but others around the table asked some pointed questions. It went on like that for a while, with four different people presenting, and Jane became increasingly aware that she still hadn't asked a question or made a point. She was just sitting there going 'Hmm' and nodding in support when everyone else did.

The CEO looked pleased with progress but had started to check her watch noticeably. 'Excellent, excellent work,' she suddenly interjected. 'Most of these changes we should have been doing for years. They all seem to either save money or make our processes faster and smarter. All great stuff. But I wonder if we need something bigger?' The CEO paused and looked around the room. 'I feel we need a truly ambitious goal for our company. And one that everyone can understand and feel enthusiastic about.'

In contrast to the earlier part of the meeting, everyone around the table was suddenly quiet and looking thoughtful. Jane could swear the CEO was now looking directly at her. And in fact, over the last half-hour an idea had begun to form in her mind. It had started when she remembered telling Ben about the wind-farm petition Aunty Em had signed. He had asked: 'If they build the wind farm close to our house, does that mean we'd get the energy in here?' Jane had been pleased he'd asked such a smart question, and they'd looked it up online together. She'd also posted about it (with a little pride) on the parenting website. The Godmother had responded very warmly:

> Well done, Ben! Yes, if you live near wind turbines, then you'll likely get some of the energy into your home. But because the UK has a national grid, we actually share the energy. So if you want more turbines, solar panels and green energy to be built, then you'd better switch to a green-energy supplier.

The Godmother

Jane and Chris had done some research, and realised they could change to a green electricity supplier without paying extra. Ben had been really pleased when they told him, and started talking about the proposed wind farm as 'his', asking: 'Will my wind farm be built soon?'

Now, thinking about Ben's enthusiasm and what she'd learned online about the importance of green energy, Jane spoke up: 'What about buying 100 per cent renewable energy for the company?' she suggested. 'There's that wind farm that might be built nearby, so local people will be interested. And it's a big idea that everyone will understand.'

The CEO leaned back in her chair. 'Well,' she said, as everyone turned from her to Jane and back again, 'that *is* a big idea. And if it's not too expensive, then I think we might have our grand goal.'

Jane grinned and decided not to mention that the company's new big idea actually came from a nine-year-old schoolboy.

7

A Good Life

The future is already here – it's just not evenly distributed yet.

—William Gibson

In 1851, the evocatively named Crystal Palace, in London, was built to hold the Great Exhibition of the Works of Industry of All Nations.

Huge taffeta dresses and long sideburns were the fashion (not on the same person, admittedly), and both were on show at the Great Exhibition. This ground-breaking and enormous show-house was the brainchild of Queen Victoria's husband, Prince Albert. And nothing like it had ever been seen before. There were 10 miles of galleries, with over 100,000 exhibits gathered from across the world, many of them wonders of the newly born industrial age, others wild and exotic. Huge printing presses could be seen under the same roof as a 50kg lump of gold from China. Visitors thrilled at railway engines, tall Egyptian statues, rooms full of porcelain and carriages, fully grown trees, a folding piano and a jewel-encrusted stuffed elephant. Huge numbers of people visited the exhibition, many of them travelling for days from tiny villages and farms across the country in groups led by their local vicars.

The Great Exhibition changed the course of history because a third of Britons had their minds blown by it, and they then went on to build the world's first industrial empire. People who had never before left their little villages, where they worked the land in much the same way their medieval ancestors had, suddenly had a vision of what the future could look like. And they wanted it. Without the Great Exhibition, I wonder how long the Industrial Revolution would have taken to begin, if it ever did.

Today we need something to blow our minds in the same way the exhibition blew those of the Victorians. We need a way to inspire a whole generation to make a future as different as the one the Victorian villagers chose.

As the London *Times* wrote at the time about the wonders on show at the Crystal Palace: 'Space and time are annihilated, and intelligence flies instantaneously between man and man at any distance, however great.' Maybe this was overstating it a bit for 1851, when it still took weeks for a letter to be shipped across the Atlantic, but the *Times* quote would be spot on today. We can have our Great Exhibition. In fact, we already have it. It's bigger and more wild and wonderful than anything Queen Victoria could have imagined. And it's called the internet.

All the happy heroes out there are sharing their stories, their inventions and hints of the future. It's a wonderful picture, and I love exploring it. Over the last decades I've found thousands of stories of happy heroes already living the future. So let me take you on a tour of the wild and wonderful world they are making.

The Great Happy Hero Exhibition

Roll up, roll up, ladies and gentlemen, and visit the Great Happy Hero Exhibition!

Gasp at this window onto the world of tomorrow. Stroll around the pavilions and tents. Take a peek at the wonders laid out before you. Be astounded, be astonished and be awed! Visit the home of the future, transform your body, marvel at gadgets, make new friends and be your own boss. This is the world of the hero!

This Great Exhibition is laid out like a giant carnival, with large tents dotted across the fields, each glittering with different colours and designs. Strange sounds, music and rumbles are coming from many of them. Magic is happening within.

As a happy hero you have a special golden ticket. Hold on to it, because it's your free pass to look inside every tent and see the world you are making.

Please, step right in…

Good Health

You are drawn to a large, bright, clean tent surrounded by luscious green grass. You notice that everyone walking out has shining eyes and a spring in their step. They seem to look rather healthier, thinner and stronger than the people walking in. And they all seem to be smiling.

Step into the Good Health Tent. The doctor will see you now…

We've already explored how working to make a difference in the world will make you healthier and less prone to illness and stress. That's all because of the psychological benefits of the 'helper's high' (see Chapter One). But there are other, very tangible benefits of the better world we happy heroes want to build. Especially when it comes to solving climate change. And one of the most surprising things about it is how it will cure us too. There is a direct link between the things scientists say we need to do to cut carbon and the beneficial knock-on effects on our health. Because so many of the causes of climate change are also causes of our modern illnesses (for example, sitting in a car all day is dreadful for both). But this is brilliant news, because it means that changing the world for the better will automatically change us too.

CLIMATE HEALTH	OUR HEALTH
Cycle and walk rather than driving	= less obesity, higher fitness and strength
Eat more locally produced food	= healthy diets, lower cancer levels
Drive less in cities	= less asthma, bronchitis and respiratory cancer
Plant and spend a lot more time around trees	= lower levels of depression, dementia and stroke
Protect natural habitats	= reduced allergies and better tolerance to viruses
Eat less saturated fat from meat	= reduced heart disease and diabetes
Produce less waste	= less heavy-metals poisoning, especially in slums

These are just a few of the most obvious positive impacts on our health of ditching climate-change-causing systems and replacing them with clean green ones. Get to this future and we'll all drop a few pounds and add a few years to our lives pretty quickly.

My own city is a good place to start. London is a beautiful, busy metropolis. It also has one of the worst air-pollution records of any city in Europe. As my young godson (who lives somewhere cleaner) pointed out on his first visit to the British capital: 'Errghh, why is my snot black?'

Getting us fat and polluted Londoners out of cars and onto bikes would make a big difference to the air in the city. A group of doctors have done the maths, and they estimate that a shift away from cars and towards walking or cycling would, for most Londoners, hit heart disease and stroke: both could fall by up to 20 per cent.[1] In a world where a billion obese people are at terrible risk of heart trouble, cycling could be a huge lifesaver. Some of the other benefits of getting us moving are even more surprising. More 'active' travel would reduce breast cancer by up to 13 per cent, dementia by over 8 per cent

1. Devtel Ganten et al., 'Health Co-Benefits of Policies to Tackle Climate Change', An Executive Summary for *The Lancet* Series 376.9755 (2010).

and even depression by about 5 per cent. That would be a beautiful gift for sufferers, and for their families.

A little further afield, greener travel in Delhi could bring a huge 25 per cent cut in heart disease and strokes, and up to a 17 per cent reduction in diabetes.[2] A massive increase in walking would cut pollution, build healthier bodies and keep those bodies safer. (The death toll on Delhi's roads is quite terrifying, and walking or cycling could cut that by a third.)

Many of us could keep living, loving and breathing for longer just by changing how we get around. It's almost as though cycling is a magic cure for modern illness. Every time a happy hero takes their bike rather than a car they are helping to cure themselves and the climate at the same time. It's an effect almost as powerful as changing how you eat.

Farming livestock, especially beef cattle, is surprisingly dirty. And I don't just mean cow pats. As I mentioned earlier, methane (from cow farts and burps) is worse for the climate than carbon dioxide. It sounds silly, but with over a billion cattle currently being raised to feed us, that is a lot of methane. Feeding, transporting and cooking all those animals makes livestock farming responsible for over 10 per cent of global greenhouse-gas emissions – even more than air travel.[3] Extra smug points for vegetarians and those happy heroes cutting down on meat. But you don't need to give up meat entirely; just cutting adult consumption of saturated fat from animal sources by a third would reduce heart disease in the population by around 15 per cent[4] in the UK. Heart disease is the stalking ghoul of modern life, snatching away far too many of us, including good friends of mine. I recommend saving the meat for when it really matters, like a proper juicy steak at the weekend, while dropping the casual meat during the week (like that nasty, antibiotic-laced, hormone-pumped slice of processed ham in your sandwich).

2. Ibid.

3. IPCC, *Climate Change 2014: Mitigation of Climate Change. Contribution of Working Group III to the Fifth Assessment Report of the Intergovernmental Panel on Climate Change* (Cambridge: Cambridge University Press, 2014).

4. Devtel Ganten et al., 'Health Co-Benefits of Policies to Tackle Climate Change', An Executive Summary for *The Lancet* Series 376.9755 (2010).

While your physical health will benefit from you being a happy hero, changing the world can also improve your mental health. There are now over 100 Green Gyms in the UK. Sign up to one and you'll be invited to local parks to help mend fences, clear weeds or plant trees. It's hard work and you'll feel your heart pumping. But the reason more doctors in the UK are allowed to prescribe joining a Green Gym is because of the psychological benefits. The government has been working with the mental-health charity MIND to study the effects of these Green Gyms on well-being, and they are confident that they help people with depression as much as medication can, because being out in nature has a proven impact on our happiness and stress levels. And it doesn't have to be the middle of a forest: just a stroll in the little local park or sitting on a bench under a tree for lunch makes a difference. As our cities become greener and less car-choked, it will become easier for all of us to catch these moments of 'nature's cure'.

And being a happy hero isn't just good for your life, it can also save the lives of others. One of the worst health threats in countries like the UK is a silent killer: loneliness, especially among older people. Over 2 million people over 65 will spend today on their own, most alone in their homes. In fact, half of older people in the UK consider TV to be their main form of company, with 17 per cent of over-65s seeing a friend or family member less than once a week.[5] It's been estimated that feeling lonely has the same impact on health and longevity as smoking, generating all the personal and NHS costs that come with it. But happy heroes can help.

'I love having Gary visit me. We can have a real laugh, which is important. You've got to have a laugh! But I think he's totally crackers for all the running he does,' says Edna, who lives alone but is signed up as a 'coach' in the GoodGym. This means that once a week Gary runs to her house, stops in for a chat and then runs home. And hundreds of other runners have ditched their gym memberships and instead run to make 20-minute visits to old people across London. For the older folk, it's a weekly lifeline to the outside world, while for

5. Susan Davidson and Phil Rossall, 'Loneliness Evidence Review', Age UK, revised July 2014.

the runners, knowing how much the visits are valued gives them the extra push to put their trainers on. It's very popular, and is now going global, because staying motivated to work-out can be a problem for many. But making a difference can be a massive feel-good reward, leaving you lighter on your feet – in more ways than one.

And now for the final extraordinary discovery in the Good Health Tent – how solving climate change cures the common cold! Well, sort of. A study in the *British Journal of Sports Medicine* of 1,000 adults reported that both the duration and severity of upper-respiratory-tract infections were lower in people who undertook more aerobic activity – including cycling and fast walking.[6]

There you have it. The best way to be healthier, happier, thinner and stronger is to save the world!

As you look around the tent you notice helpful-looking folk are wandering around with clipboards and a smile. They want to help get you involved. Let's see what's on their menu…

The Happy Hero's Handbook

In Chapter 4, 'Learning Heroism', you started your Happy Hero Action Plan. And perhaps you've already taken some action. Now you can add some specific organisations and links to use what you've learned.

Start Cycling and Walking

If you haven't cycled in a long time (or if you're planning to bike in a city), then get some training in first. In the UK you can sign up to bikeability.org.uk. This is a government-run site to help you find quick training. I also love Sustrans.org, who map out all the cycle routes across the country and give loads of advice on getting started.

6. Nieman D. C., Henson D. A., Austin M. D., *et al.*, 'Upper respiratory tract infection is reduced in physically fit and active adults', *British Journal of Sports Medicine*, 2011 (45:987-992).

One of my favourite apps for walking is Walkit. With lots of different cities covered, it shows you the fastest (and most pleasant) way to walk between points, rather than driving or getting a bus. More apps and tools are being developed daily (I just spotted a 'walking map' of the London Tube), so keep looking.

Eat Better

Want to cut down on meat, but not cut it out? Across the world people are joining in with Meatless Mondays. You can too, by making a pledge to start each week as a vegetarian. Find your country's unique site (with advice, events and recipes) at meatless-monday.com.

Change Lives

The GoodGym (Goodgym.org) and the Green Gym (Greengym.org) – are incredible ways to make a difference to yourself and the world. I promise they are also great fun (and very welcoming to beginners).

Feel Good

Finally, one action that doesn't need a website or app – the outdoors! Every happy hero needs to recharge, and green spaces seem to have an extra boosting power for that. In the next 24 hours try and spend at least 30 minutes in a local park, on a beach or under some trees, or just eat your lunch on a bench by a tree. Let nature do its thing.

Good Jobs

You've now got a spring in your step and a glint in your eye from the Good Health Tent. And you're ready to explore the Great Happy Hero Exhibition a little more.

Wander further along and your eye may be caught by crowds of very busy people. Walk closer and you'll notice they are busy people making money. And they are all looking rather happy about it.

Most of us wouldn't be surprised to hear that people who work in service to others – in healthcare, the emergency services, teaching, overseas aid, etc. – all report the highest sense of 'meaning' and 'purpose' in the work they do. Today more and more of us are seeking the same. And not just in the jobs traditionally associated with helping people, but in any work that we do.

Thankfully, building the happy-hero future is going to require the creation of many more meaningful jobs, because all those wind turbines, solar panels, cycle lanes and new ways of eating, travelling and having fun are going to need to be designed, built and sold. It will be the largest transformation in the economy humanity has ever pulled off.

Some of those jobs are already here. The US Department of Energy announced that in 2016, solar energy companies employed more people in the US than all their coal, gas and oil plants combined. And in Germany, the largest renewable-energy employer in the European Union, the field of renewable energy supports over 370,000 jobs.[7] That's close to the number of Germans already employed in car manufacturing.

New happy-hero jobs are growing and developing across the world. In Bangladesh, over a million poor rural families now have energy thanks to small solar panels provided by the charity Grameen Shakti. That's amazing – not only for the families, but also for those who build, sell, replace and manage the panels, the existence of which has created new permanent jobs for several thousand women and some 60,000 young people in managing, servicing and selling the energy.

Listed below are other real 'new jobs' with too few people trained for them, causing wars between employers over a limited talent pool. They are well paid, purposeful jobs, in need of bright people ready to get started:

7. Yi Xu, 'Fact Sheet: Jobs in Renewable Energy and Energy Efficiency (2014)', EESI – Environmental and Energy Study Institute, n.p., 23 December 2014.

- Bicycle-fleet technician
- Carbon trader
- Green-building architect
- Eco-travel consultant
- Recycling manager
- Ethical-fashion purchasing manager
- Organic-brand manager
- Energy auditor
- Pollution-control specialist
- Solar installer
- Turbine-factory worker
- Vertical farmer
- Wildlife biologist
- Fish warden
- Hydrologist
- High-speed-rail conductor
- Insulation installer
- Geothermal engineer
- Ethical-finance advisor
- Smart-grid planner
- Hybrid-car mechanic
- Algae-oil producer
- Fuel-cell technician
- Chief sustainability officer

Many of these jobs might sound a bit strange (just like being a 'coder' in the IT industry used to), but they are growing professions you can train for. Watch out for them, train for them and prepare your kids for a career in them – not least because they pay well. In the UK the average salary in the renewable-energy industry is over £45,000. And according to the Totaljobs recruitment website in January 2017, that average salary rose by 10 per cent compared to the previous year.[8] I don't know many other jobs in which you can expect a 10 per cent raise in only 12 months.

And as these jobs have started to multiply, so has another part of the economy. It's a part I've been working in for decades, and it's called 'social enterprise'. Last year 5 per cent of all businesses in the UK were classed as social enterprises – all working to solve social or environmental problems. According to the UK Cabinet Office, they contribute over £20 billion to the economy and employ nearly 1 million people. One of my favourite things about social enterprises isn't just that they make a difference, but that 40 per cent of them are led by women (compared to only 18 per cent of regular small businesses). A lot of these new companies are 'Benefit Corporations', or B-corps,

8. 'What Is the Average Salary for Renewable Energy Jobs?' Totaljobs.com, n.p., March 2017.

a global standard for certifying companies that try to make a difference in everything they do. These are companies like Warby Parker, who donate a pair of glasses in the developing world every time you buy one, or Ben & Jerry's (one of the largest B-corps), and even Roshan, a telecoms company that is now the largest private employer in Afghanistan. All these and more are growing, profitable and purposeful businesses. In fact, I predict these will become some of the most successful businesses in the next few decades, all proving that 'doing good is good business'. And they all need smart, passionate, hard-working happy heroes just like you.

It feels amazing to work for a better world, because it's work you can feel proud of. New research shows that at the end of the work day, if you strongly feel that your work has made a positive difference to other people's lives, you'll feel happier at bedtime.[9]

A few years ago I met some school kids who were working with volunteers on a green project. These kids, from a private girls' school, were bright-eyed and enthusiastic, and so, uplifted by their energy, I decided to volunteer as a class mentor myself.

Running slightly late from a business meeting and trotting along in high heels and carrying a briefcase, I turned up on my first day at the local school I'd been allocated, all fired up for a roomful of bright young things. But I hadn't been assigned to a private girls' school. There were grilles and locks on most of the doors, and the rooms were all bare and badly lit. Nevertheless, undaunted, I looked around the scruffy classroom in which I was meeting my charges: a group of south London teenagers warily eyeing the fumbling white chick who'd come to talk to them about saving the world. It was like something out of a naff 1980s movie.

Thankfully, I'd come prepared. Not with wisdom, a heart of gold or a will of steel, but with biscuits. And not shoddy biscuits either: proper posh, American-style cookies, heavy on the chocolate – and lots of them. We talked about biscuits. We talked about school. We talked about what it's like being a woman in business. We talked

9. Sabine Sonnentag and Adam M. Grant, 'Doing Good at Work Feels Good at Home, but Not Right Away: When and Why Perceived Prosocial Impact Predicts Positive Affect', *Personnel Psychology*, 65: 495–530.

about being a kid in central London. We talked about saving the world, and their feelings about global issues and inequalities they'd already experienced closer to home.

Every week I brought the biscuits and we talked. By the end of term we'd run some great green projects and had reached a clear conclusion about the world: we'd decided that everyone is basically the same, from teenagers to grown women, when it comes to chocolate-cookie appreciation. But one thing about my life totally blew them away for the whole time we worked together, and that was how much I loved my job – because most of them had never met anyone who did. Not their parents, aunts or uncles, family friends and, seemingly, not even their teachers. As far as they were concerned, the only point in working was to make money. And my experience of working at something I loved, something I was proud of, something that I knew made a difference shocked the hell out of them. They hadn't realised that was an option.

I look forward to them applying for jobs with Futerra in a few years' time. Or perhaps they'll hire me instead.

The Happy Hero's Handbook

In the Good Jobs tent you're beckoned over to the 'Happy Hero Career Fair', to find out how you're going to make a living by making the world a better place…

Become an Intrapreneur

As Dr Martin Luther King Jr declared: 'No work is insignificant.' The best place for a happy hero to start making a difference is in the job they already have. You don't always need a new job in order to do meaningful work.

There's a new word for people who try to make their current workplaces better: 'intrapreneur'. Intrapreneurs set up Sustainability Champions groups, they start a recycling scheme, they organise volunteering days, and they ask questions about how their business is going to make a difference. Some of the happiest heroes I know are people who are changing their workplaces from the inside.

Become a Do-Gooder

Some happy heroes want to make the jump into a full-time career in social or environmental change. There are more and more jobs available, and websites like idealist.org are a great place to start. There are thousands of full-time, part-time and volunteering roles available, in everything from leadership to administrative work, and including roles in which you can get out into the world, meet people and really see the difference you are making.

Become a Social Entrepreneur

Or perhaps you want to go the whole way and set up a social enterprise. There are lots of grants and advice available (in fact, my company, Futerra, was originally helped by a grant). Check out unltd.org.uk in the UK, or the B-corp movement at bcorporation.net. Amazing networks and events for social entrepreneurs are run across the world – just search #SocEnt for updates.

But whatever you do, when you wake up tomorrow morning, think: How can I make my work matter today? I promise that when you go to bed, you'll feel better for it.

Good Homes

When my friend Dermot set up his 'green home' company, he was searching for a great selling point. He planned to refurbish homes with good insulation, draught proofing and even a touch of renewable energy: buy a 'make-my-home-green' makeover and you can expect lower bills and a slashed carbon footprint. Important, yes, but not quite the killer advertising message Dermot was looking for. So he asked around. He visited homes that had amazing insulation and ones that leaked energy out and let draughts in. He totted up people's bills and drank cups of tea on their sofas. And he found it – the ultimate reason why your home needs a green-energy makeover.

The answer? Sex.

We all know sex is supposed to sell. But it seems sex can sell rolls of insulation as well as fast cars, because in cold houses people walk about from bedroom to bathroom and back wrapped up in floor-length fluffy robes, flannel pyjamas and thick socks. In a cold and draughty British home, a couple might not see each other naked from October till May. It turns out warm homes are sexier homes. Best green selling point ever.

And warm and frisky partners are just one of the wonders you can see in the home-of-tomorrow exhibit.

This part of the Great Happy Hero Exhibition is a little different to the other tents. A whole set of real houses has been set up, and they are open for you to look around. So walk through the green and sunny parkland to a red-brick house with a glinting roof. Meet me at the doorway. I'm smartly dressed, eager and carrying a clipboard. I'm going to be your Estate Agent for this visit…

Come in, do come in. Lovely day, isn't it? Just take a moment to notice how green the front garden is. Very thick and lush. It's been planted with heat-resistant, water-saving plants. Terribly smart, and it means you can expect a green welcome when you come home – rather better than that brown, parched look that so many gardens have these days.

I'm sure you noticed the lovely solar panels on the way in. Most of the roof is made with them. They are so easy to maintain, and they produce energy and lashings of hot water for baths. Plus, this property has under-floor heating throughout – all from just those panels. Amazing, eh?

You ask how do solar panels work in England? I know we suffer from a little bit of bad weather now and then, but don't worry, modern panels are extremely efficient and actually benefit from a few clouds, which bounce the sunshine back again. And a 'wood-chip generator' has been installed for when the weather is really grim. With all the solar energy you'll be selling back to the grid during summer, the boiler actually works out as almost free to run.

And, of course, this sought-after property is super-efficient. Just like those new supercars, this home comes with an on-board computer. Sensors around the house are all linked to a thermostat, which opens and closes windows to regulate the heat and cold for a perfect temperature.

Pardon? Oh yes, sir, of course you can override it and open windows yourself.

Madam, I see you're appreciating the wood panelling. Gorgeous, isn't it? Turns out that wood is excellent for insulation, and, of course, all the wood in the house is sourced sustainably. If you like natural surfaces, perhaps you'd like a peek in the loft? It's lined with lamb's wool. Yes, actual lamb's wool. Sheep grow the best insulation possible. No, madam, I'm afraid I don't think it's available in cashmere.

Behind all that glamorous cladding you'll find something a little higher tech. The previous owners stripped back all the old plaster and installed 'space-blanket' insulation before putting in the wood. This house isn't a new build; it's a refit of an older property all upgraded to the latest eco standards. The gorgeous light that's flooding the hallway comes from operable skylights in the stairwell and the sitting room downstairs. They are terribly smart and allow for natural, passive ventilation on hot days, while the orientation of the glass has been carefully set to make the most of the sun's heat when it's chilly.

It's so efficient you can basically heat this entire house with a hair dryer. No more flannel pyjamas for you, sir [winking at madam, knowingly].

The previous owners enjoyed the 'comfort of the house because it's cool in summer, warm in winter', and all the insulation makes it 'quiet even though the main road is there'.

Perhaps you'd like to step upstairs? Yes, madam, it does smell lovely, doesn't it? The whole house is painted internally with smart, natural paints. You can let a child play in the same room while you're painting – no smells, no fumes. In fact, the paint even absorbs toxins and carbon from the air and cleans your home's atmosphere. All helped by these [dramatically throwing open a door to reveal a room divided by 'living walls' of grasses and small, luscious green plants]. These gorgeous green screens are really alive. Go on, give them a stroke. Those are living plants and dwarf shrubs on a lightweight frame. They only require a little water. You can move them around to create different spaces and light effects in the room. They really are a selling feature of the home. I've had a lot of interest from other potential buyers, I can tell you.

From here you can see that part of the lower roof is covered in sedum grass. It's almost as good an insulator as wool and attracts butterflies. Adds that English-countryside ambience right here in the city, doesn't it?

It also helps the roof catch rainwater to flush the loo. Ridiculous that we pay our taxes to purify water to drinking quality and then we just flush it away, especially when here in England we tend to produce enough free water from the sky, don't we [twinkly laugh]?

I hope you noticed the full garage? Of course, it comes with an electric charger for your car. With all the green energy you're producing you'll never have to pay for petrol again, I suspect. Just let her charge while you sleep.

Are you looking for a long- or short-term let? Because if you kept this home in the family, in about 30 years' time, if the previous occupants have got their sums right, the excess electricity flowing from this house into the grid will have cancelled out all of the carbon costs of building it, leaving a non-existent footprint on the earth's resources.

Of course, one of the most innovative aspects of this place isn't the house itself, but the community-owned space it has access to. As the previous owners say in the brochure, the 'social side is spectacularly good', and with a 'nice community spirit, it's non-isolating'.

No, sir, I don't mean some sort of 1960s hippie commune. This is more like those posh private gardens local residents have the key for in central London squares. Because as well as this home, you are also buying access to group-owned meeting spaces, play areas for children, offices and a gym. There's even a storage space where you can lend and borrow tools and other costly equipment you might not need all the time. That includes 3D printers, as well as power drills. There's even a weekly meal everyone brings something to, just like a street party. I suppose it's no surprise the previous owners say they actually 'like their neighbours'.

That lovely park and garden space you walked through to reach the house also belongs to this community. You'll have a claim on all of that, including the large fruit and vegetable patches. Makes it a little easier to stay fit, doesn't it, sir, if you're growing and eating your own veggies? Access to resources like that means you're almost 40 per cent less likely to be overweight, according to studies. Yes, madam, you are more likely to lose weight through having greenery nearby than by joining a slimming club.

The previous owners weren't tree huggers. As they said themselves, 'We have never been especially conscious about environmental issues, but my wife often asked, "Why don't they invent something new?" And this is definitely something new.'

Sir, madam, are you interested in making an offer? I have several other couples visiting this afternoon [holding out a clipboard to sign]...

The Happy Hero's Handbook

Back in the real world, all this stuff turns out to be available right now. All the technology outlined above actually exists, and lots of people already enjoy it in their homes. The direct quotes are from people who live in green homes right now. Of course, it does all sound pretty pricey (if pretty nice). But remember that a little bit goes a long way.

Join a Transition Town

The folks over at transitionnetwork.org help whole communities move in this direction. It's really worth checking out whether there's a group where you live. And if not, maybe start one!

Energise Your Home

Governments are starting to offer grants and schemes to make solar panels and insulation more affordable. The Energy Saving Trust keeps an updated list of all the ways to find funding in the UK: visit energysavingtrust.org.uk.

Other parts of the story, like the community space, anyone can organise. And if you've got a tech-savvy teenager at home, then linking up cheap sensors to your laptop to regulate your heating is simple – or just get a modern energy monitor.

Grow for Good

While you might not have a huge garden, you can grow things just about anywhere. My friend Ed gets an impressive crop of herbs and veggies from pots on his windowsills in his fourth-floor flat in Brixton. He makes an incredible salsa from the tomatoes and chillies he grows year round!

A happy hero's home is one of the best places to start taking action – and one of the nicest ways to enjoy the rewards.

Good Travel

Buzzing between the tents at the exhibition are vehicles weird and wonderful, large and small. There's even a sleek silver airship tethered above the fields at one end.

The new cars, bikes and everything in between are impressive technology. But sometimes a simple solution can change as much as a new invention. During the Christmas holidays in 1998, a student was trying to get home from university. He didn't have a car of his own but needed to transport presents (and some dirty laundry, I suspect), so wondered if anyone from his uni was heading the same way he was. He posted a handwritten message on a noticeboard and got two offers of a lift. On the drive home, as he and the driver chatted and shared the fuel cost, the idea for his business was born. Liftshare now has over 400,000 members across the UK using his app and website to coordinate and book a car share. Lots of people use it for their commute, regular hospital trips for the elderly or even to get to the Glastonbury festival!

This is what being a happy hero is all about: finding smart and easy ways to make a difference, and perhaps even getting a bit of carpool karaoke into the bargain.

I love travel. Or at least I love visiting different countries and experiencing the cultures, spectacles and adventures you can find far from home. I also don't mind a few weeks on a beach with a glass of something exotic either. But the act of being strapped down in a pressurised metal sausage and told when I can use the bathroom, listening to people snore and babies wail, and eating off plastic plates is just unpleasant. There must be a better way. That's where the pressure to solve climate change can fuel innovation. And one of the best ideas to improve our travel is actually an update of an old one: airships. There are some huge, modern airships already being tested, and I can't wait for them to offer a passenger service. Airships fly much lower than airplanes, so they don't need pressurised cabins. No more breathing reused air, and more walking about on the deck outside. Personally, I'd love to leave London at 11am on a Thursday, glide across the Atlantic and arrive in New York for lunch on Friday with minimal jet lag and feeling rested. Count me in for airship travel.

Of course, the first thing to be moved around by airship probably won't be people but the approximately 80 million tonnes of cargo we put into the air every year. FedEx is already considering this, mainly because airship transport costs today are half that of airplane cargo, and all with a tiny carbon footprint by comparison.

But airships aren't the only big innovation in our skies. In 2015, a huge aircraft with a wingspan wider than that of a Boeing 747 took off from Abu Dhabi and didn't touch down again for 23 days – because across those wings were 17,000 solar cells. The *Solar Impulse 2* was the first fuel-less plane to circumvent the globe. Speaking to journalists when he landed, one of the two pilots, Bertrand Piccard, said: 'It is a very, very special moment – it has been 15 years that I am working on this goal... I hope people will understand that it is not just a first in the history of aviation, but also a first in the history of energy.'

And travel solutions can be found everywhere, even at the heart of 'petrol-head' car racing. When 20 electric racing cars lined up on the grid for a race through the centre of Beijing in September 2014, there was a lot of cynicism that it was only a publicity stunt. The Formula One organisers had launched a new Formula E race for all-electric cars, with names like Senna, Prost and Piquet behind the wheel, teams such as Andretti, Renault and Virgin Racing, and team owners like Leonardo DiCaprio. But the race turned out to be a runaway success, with over 190 million people in more than 100 countries around the world tuning in to watch the inaugural season. Today Formula E races through streets in the hearts of major global cities, from Moscow to London. The electric cars are still a little slower than the fossil-fuel ones, but they are catching up every year. And the races are arguably more exciting, not least because they are held in city centres rather than on racetracks. Veteran race commentator Jack Nicholls sums up the energy in E-racing as: 'F1 is chess at 200mph, whereas Formula E is dodgems at 100mph.'

And electric cars aren't just for racers. According to the International Energy Agency, in 2015, the number of electric cars on the road globally passed the 1 million threshold for the first time. And, in the same year, China became the world's largest electric-car market. If you've never driven one, I encourage you to give them a try, if only for the acceleration, which can be so intense that Tesla named a hyped-up version of theirs 'insane mode'.

From electric cars to high-speed rail, there is a whole host of ways to move about faster, more cleanly and more easily than by setting petrol alight in a combustion engine. Plus, the low-carbon, happy-hero options also turn out to be cheaper and less stressful ways to get around.

A bit of lateral thinking can even turn moving itself into energy. A simple rubber paving slab has been invented by a little company called Pavegen. When pedestrians walk on it, their footfalls generate energy. Kinetic power is then stored and should be enough in busy parts of town to power street lights. Bright thinking.

The Happy Hero's Handbook

Like any good car dealer, the Good Travel tent offers you a test-drive of the new electric cars, airships and even solar-powered planes. I won't list resources for these because when it comes to electric cars, especially, there's likely to be a lot of new ones launching in the next few years.

Get Some Carpool Karaoke

Whether you've got a car or not, I really recommend Lift-share.com or your national equivalent. Everyone is fully vetted beforehand and the cost savings can really stack up. Check if your company has its own car-share scheme you can join.

Let the Train Take the Strain

One of the best ways to get around is by train. Even though rail fares are sometimes far too high, it's still possible to find great bargains. I use loco2.com to find tickets for travel right across Europe. I love taking the sleeper train down to my parents in Italy. Sleeper trains have an 'old world' glamour and there's nothing like falling asleep to the sound of the train on the tracks.

Volunteer Your Vacation

Of course, there's also lots you can do once you've reached your destination. In the last few years Volunteer Vacations have become very popular. These combine ways to make a difference with ways to unwind. You might spend your mornings teaching local kids English, and afternoons enjoying the sun on the beach. So many charities around the world would welcome your skills, even for a few weeks. Check out ResponsibleTravel.com or Earthwatch.org for inspiration.

You're almost at the end of your tour of the future, and I hope you've got a few extra ideas for your Happy Hero Action List. But just before you go, perhaps you'd like to visit the gift shop?

Good Stuff

Groups of people are walking towards the biggest tent of all. As you push back the curtain to enter, you glimpse a cornucopia of wonderful and seemingly magical stuff piled high in every corner. It looks like a genie's bazaar – and it's the gift shop for this entire fantastical exhibition.

Now, too much stuff isn't necessarily a good thing. But in this shop there's no plastic tat, no rubbish, nothing from a sweatshop or that uses up resources we don't have. And while some of us already have too much stuff, far too many people around the world don't have enough. So this tent also includes smart and life-changing stuff that can help billions of families in need. And some of it doesn't even look like stuff at all. Let's peruse the genie's wares and read the little labels on the shelves of his store…

Stuff from Stuff

Do you remember ever making a rocket out of a plastic washing-up bottle, or a doll's car out of a shoe box? If you do, then you've already 'upcycled'.

It's a simple idea and millions are already doing it: taking things that would have been thrown away and instead mending, adding to and improving them. For years people have been buying old furniture and sprucing it up for resale. Now they are doing it with everything from old clothes to entire homes. There's a massive online community of upcyclers, many of them making a good living out of smartening up and reselling former trash. In many cases, what they make is even more beautiful and useful than the original. In Japan the custom of fixing what's broken to improve it is actually centuries old. The art of *kintsugi* is a way of fixing broken pottery (bowls, cups or plates usually) with a special lacquer dusted with gold. The result is an old bowl held together by beautiful seams of gold glinting in the cracks. Upcycling at its classiest.

Big companies are also getting in on the act. You can buy a pair of trainers or jeans upcycled from plastic cleared out of the ocean. And I've worked with big brewing companies who use the leftover grain from beer production to make bread. Not only does the brewing process add protein to the grain, the bread also tastes delicious (although not of beer, unfortunately).

There is even a huge effort to upcycle all that carbon we've pumped into the atmosphere. Today it's possible to make plastic products from excess carbon sucked out of the atmosphere. More and more companies are getting interested in this process, so watch out for products 'made of air' coming soon.

Plugless Stuff

Another way to make stuff better is simply to stick a solar panel on it – not least on all our electronic equipment like laptops, tablets and mobile phones, which all look sleek and portable until you realise you must lug a different power cable around with each one. Thankfully, solar-powered gadgets are already here.

At gadget fairs you can test new laptops with built-in solar panels. These will stay powered for a full day in the park – longer than most laptops already on the market. There is also a prototype Japanese solar-powered phone, the face of which is made up of really tiny solar panels. The photovoltaic cells are virtually transparent because they are so thin. Just leave your phone face-up when you're not using it to charge.

It seems appropriate that our most modern tech will soon be powered by modern energy. High-tech solar panels and sleek white wind turbines aesthetically complement our modern tablets and smartphones much better than an old-fashioned, dirty coal power station.

I'm a gadget geek and can't wait for all these sun-chargeable gizmos. But I know that for some people solar-powered stuff isn't just about fun, but fundamental improvements in their lives.

The Maasai people burn charcoal in stoves for heat and cooking. They are among the 3 billion people[10] who rely on wood, animal waste or basic kerosene to cook and warm themselves. And a three-pack-a-day smoking habit is nothing compared to the lung pollution these fuels cause. You can see the soot and heavy particles hanging in the air. I had never had to choose between the health risk of holding my breath versus the health risk of breathing until I was welcomed into a Maasai round hut. Eyes streaming and lungs heaving, I wanted to grab the young Maasai kids in the room and carry them out into the fresh air, but they were trying to do their homework by firelight. All that soot works its way into lungs and kills people, especially women. According to the US Environmental Protection Agency, almost 4 million people per year are killed around the world by cooking on these old-fashioned stoves.[11] The kerosene lamps that people use are worse. They are like having a petrol bomb in your home that threatens to explode at any point. All of this is creating huge amounts of carbon too. While each fire itself is tiny compared to running a car in London, the billions of them combined have a serious climate-change impact.

All this can be solved with a bit of tin foil. A simple foil solar cooker can save millions of trees, save millions of lives and, I'm told, save marriages, by keeping husbands indoors (because they don't leave to escape smog and soot!).

Even basic clay can change lives. In Haiti, a young entrepreneur called Duquesne Fednard started making efficient clay cooking stoves to sell cheaply to families to replace old charcoal burners. They use about a third of the fuel, cook food even faster and are much cleaner. They also look nice and save space, which is helpful if your home is a small hut. Duquesne is a pretty incredible guy who built his business using student loans and charm, and so managed to open a small factory in Port-au-Prince, manufacturing the stoves and saving lives.

10. *Energy Technology Perspectives 2016: Towards Sustainable Urban Energy Systems* (Paris: OECD/IEA, 2016).

11. Practical Action, *Poor People's Energy Outlook 2010* (Rugby, UK, 2010).

He was already a happy hero in my book, but when I met him I learned the story of what happened next. Just weeks after his factory was opened, the devastating earthquake hit and, like so much else in Haiti, his new factory was flattened and everything he had built was lost. But Duquesne and his team chose to go on, knowing that their clay stoves were needed more than ever in the earthquake's aftermath. They moved into large, draughty tents provided by the UN and kept on making the stoves, as queues of women lined up to buy them in every village they visited.

Then Hurricane Sandy hit Haiti and tore everything down once again. Duquesne explained with a wry smile how they patched up the torn tents, grieved for those lost and carried right on making the stoves, next to the rubble of their factory. I met Duquesne in London when he was receiving an Ashden Award for his efforts. I'm not ashamed to say I wept as he went up and collected his honour. He's quite the happy hero.

The Stuff Machine

In 2014, NASA emailed a ratchet wrench to the International Space Station.

Of course, technically, they just emailed the blueprint for the wrench. The astronauts then 'printed' out the tool itself on a 3D printer.

You've probably heard of 3D printers already (or, to given them their formal title, which I prefer because it sounds like 1980s sci-fi, 'atomic synthesisers'). They work by building up layer upon layer of material to make a product, in the same way you'd build up a brick wall or a coil clay pot, but with each layer sometimes only micrometres thick. The early versions only worked with plastic. But today 3D printers are building with cloth (someone made a teddy bear) and even food (including chocolate). I have a belt buckle that was 3D printed which I'm immensely proud of. But the 3D printer took over an hour to print something that would be punched out in a factory in seconds. So why all the excitement?

3D printing is already making things (like microscopic medical equipment) that you can't make any other way. But the real transformation will come as they get faster and smarter, because then you could just print out everything you need in your own home – a dress, a pizza, a spare part for your bike (perhaps even the bike itself). Shops won't have to waste enormous amounts of resources keeping things that you might want to buy in stock, often having to wastefully landfill whatever isn't sold. The only things that are made by the 3D printer would be the things you actually want.

Then things get even more exciting, because your 3D printer still needs raw materials from which to make your stuff. But imagine a 3D 'breaker' sitting alongside your 3D 'maker'. When you're finished with something, you simply pop it into the breaker, which disassembles the molecules and holds them ready for the next thing you want to make.

Today the global market for 3D-printing filaments is estimated to be worth around $531 million, which inspired three engineering students at the University of British Columbia in Canada to invent the ProtoCycler – a device that can grind up all kinds of plastic waste into a beautiful clean spool of plastic filament to be used in a 3D printer. We're talking anything here – plastic bottles, 3D-printing cut-offs, takeaway food containers. It works a little like a juicer and is making the vision of eco-friendly 3D printing a reality.

The future of stuff is making only exactly what we want, when we want it, then breaking it down to make more stuff immediately. No waste, no crap filling up the garage. 3D printing can be the ultimate in recycling right in your home. Imagine what you'll make, and perhaps what you'll invent. Stuff will never be the same again.

Hopefully nor will you. This mini-tour of the Great Happy Hero Exhibition has just been a taste of the changes that are coming (and some that are already here). I hope you found some you'll enjoy and that you're inspired to find even more in the days, weeks and lifetime to come.

The Happy Hero's Handbook

There are so many amazing new products being invented every

day that it's difficult to pick just a few for this section! Instead, I've compiled a list (which is constantly updated) of the most exciting new products, gizmos and tools to change your life at www.thehappyhero.org.

*

The Story of a Happy Hero

'I'll just wait in the car,' Jane's dad said, a little huffily.

'Oh, c'mon, Grandad,' Ben replied, pulling at his sleeve. 'They're going to talk about my wind farm!'

'Don't worry, Ben,' Aunty Em teased. 'My brother is just an old grumpy-guts. Your mum, dad and I will come in with you and leave him out here alone.'

Jane was pleased when her dad succumbed to the pressure and hauled himself out of the car to join the family. 'Better come to keep an eye on you,' was all he said.

'Well, this is a bit of a change for us,' Chris whispered to her as they walked towards the town hall, 'but I'm rather liking my new world-changing wife.'

Jane smiled and realised that just a few months ago it would never have occurred to her to turn up at a big community meeting like this. Things really had changed.

There were a lot of people in the town hall. And up on a platform at the front were their local MP, a few men in suits and a lady in a green T-shirt who was looking around the room with interest. As everyone took their seats, one of the suited men began: 'If everyone could quieten down, please. Thank you. We're here today for a public session on the proposed installation of six wind turbines. The wind-farm development would be 4 miles west of town. You can see it here on this chart. And while the landowners and people living closest have agreed to this, others have raised objections. This is a chance for everyone's voice to be heard.'

Ben was still sitting up straight next to her, but Jane worried that the meeting might be a bit beyond him. As various of the suited men stood up, even she began to get lost in their arguments about 'higher primary cost plus ancillary costs of mitigating irregular intermittency'.

No one had spoken about the golf course, climate change or local people since it all started. Until the lady in the green T-shirt suddenly interrupted the men in suits. 'Look, we've collected over 300 signatures in support of wind energy. I've got them right here,' she said, waving a stack of papers. 'Shouldn't we be talking about climate change here? I'm from the People's Climate Group and I just want to say that this comes down to corporate greed versus children's futures. You're money-grabbing at the climate's expense!'

Jane could practically feel her dad's frowning 'harrumph' from further down the aisle. And she realised that a lot of other people in the room who had been bored before were now looking at the green lady with distinctly unfriendly expressions.

'Now, now.' Finally their local MP spoke up. 'We don't need to get hysterical about all this. The way I see it' – he leaned back in his chair with a big smile – 'is that perhaps now isn't the right time. I'm not against all this wind-energy stuff per se. I just think we should wait for other towns to test it out first, ones with less to lose than us.' He smiled confidently out over the room. 'Just put the planning permission on hold for, say, 18 months? Then see where we are.'

A lot of the suits on the stage started nodding sagely, and Jane realised most of the room had joined in, especially her dad, and even Chris was making his 'fair point' face. She turned to Aunty Em, but she was sitting calmly with a smile, and when she caught Jane's eye she just gave a little encouraging nod.

But Jane didn't know what to do. Ben was looking bewildered beside her. And up on the stage the green lady was arguing with one of the suits, while the others spoke to the MP. As if receiving some signal, the MP got to his feet and said: 'None of us want someone coming from London to tell us what to do now, do we?' He waved a hand dismissively towards the green lady and went on: 'This is a local issue for us local folk to decide. And until there's agreement, I propose – and it's been formally seconded by these gentlemen behind me – that we indefinitely delay planning permission for this so-called wind farm until things become clearer.' His last words were delivered with such finality that a few of the men on the platform, and some of the audience, started clapping.

Jane's heart sank. If someone didn't do something soon, then Ben's wind farm would be lost for ever.

8

Our Future

The future belongs to those who believe in the beauty of their dreams.

—Eleanor Roosevelt

Together we've already discovered that some things we *have* to do, we should really *want* to do. We've got our heads screwed back on and we're going to work together to save the world and reap our rewards.

Have you started to act heroically yet? Even in a small way? If so, you should have experienced that shot of heightened self-esteem as payback. And now I want you to become addicted to that feeling and to seek bigger and bigger buzzes. Because being a happy hero is a lifelong journey – and that life will be longer, happier and a lot more fun if you use it to change the world.

Everything I've shown you is already happening and available to you today, but now I want to go a little further, to step into the future and give a mere hint of what might be to come.

I want the future that's beyond this crisis curve so badly. But I'll be careful not to sound too science-fictiony, because that's not what this is about. It is about being ambitious – the massive, super, need-a-little-lie-down-to-recover type of ambitious.

We know what being bad looks like: negativity and denial, fear, guilt and climate change. No way are we letting that happen. We know what being blind is like: cheating and ignoring our issues, trying to fix a new problem with some very old tools, delaying the breakdown for a while, but spiralling downwards eventually. We aren't that stupid either.

Instead, we're going to be bright and climb our crisis curve to a smarter and happier world. Billions of us have got to climb it – to pull, heave and give each other a push up. It's going to get scary. We're going to scrape our knees, we're going to struggle and wobble, but we'll keep going. We'll get tired, our legs will shake with the effort, and we'll wonder if we're going to fall as we climb up this curve. Then someone beside us, someone unexpected, just as tired as us, will grab our collar and drag us to the next handhold.

It will feel like it's never going to end.

But we'll pull, climb, keep going.

Keep going.

Then – BAM – our hands will reach over the top.

And if we do all of that, if we work that hard, then we get to be a Type 1 Planet.

A Type 1 Planet

Type 1 is an uninspiring term for an incredible idea. In 1964, a Soviet astronomer called Nikolai Kardashev wrote an article about the search for extraterrestrial civilisations. Humans had just begun to reach for the stars, and we hoped we might find someone out there. Kardashev suggested a way we might spot them. He thought we should search for energy signals: not communication signals or messages, but for signs that other intelligent life had managed to break through their energy glass ceiling and into a state of abundant power.

Kardashev neatly fitted the possibilities we should search for into three types: Type 1 civilisations would harness all of the energy of their home planet; a Type 2 civilisation would get out into space and harvest all of the power of its sun and solar system; and a super-advanced Type 3 civilisation could master the energy from its entire galaxy. This method of measuring technological progress is now called the Kardashev scale.

Type 1 planets would be little shining dots of light in the dark sky, Type 2s a solar-system-sized civilisation, and Type 3s would be so large, so complex and so unimaginable, we probably couldn't tell the difference between that civilisation and a normal galaxy. Anything below Type 1 would be so young, so early in development that it wouldn't give off an energy signal strong enough for us to see at all. It would still be burning fossil fuels. Sound like anywhere you know? The rungs leading up to Type 1 have been worked out by Michael Shermer of Claremont Graduate University, and they tell an incredible story. In fact, they tell the whole story of humanity, including the next few chapters in history that we haven't got to yet. I've adapted them a little for happy heroism. See if you can spot where we are right now?

- **Type 0.1:** simple groups of pre-humans living sparsely. Technology consists of stone tools.
- **Type 0.2:** we become roaming hunter-gatherers. 'Society' begins to emerge through wider family and kinship groups.
- **Type 0.3:** people begin to farm. Family groups become tribes and settle down into little villages. Politics and skilled jobs begin to emerge. Burning wood, peat and animal waste is still the most powerful energy source – to cook with, to light the night, to drive away predators.
- **Type 0.4:** the tribes become little kingdoms, usually with a dominant leader at the top, and a class system emerges. Some people work to produce food and support a small minority of leaders. The lower classes also gather wood and dung for the fires. Domesticated animals add their labour to the energy mix.
- **Type 0.5:** the kingdoms become early states with clear territory to protect. War is born to defend those boundaries. Trade emerges between states. Complex politics and hierarchies begin and social rules dominate. Society can support artists, engineers, priests and whole groups of specialists. Some people own each other. Wood is still the main energy source and is harvested on a large scale. Mills powered by rivers and wind are added to the energy mix.
- **Type 0.6:** the era of empires. Huge groups of people are bound together by the state rather than by kinship ties. Energy is vitally important and huge efforts in trade, farming and industry go towards supporting the energy demand of the empires. Coal, basic oils and other new energy sources fuel more complex societies.

- **Type 0.7:** democracies tentatively begin, offering the vote to some people. Markets develop, and trade and war rule how societies interact with each other. War over energy sources are common as humanity's hunger for energy grows. It is needed to fuel innovation and power trade. Energy allows for leisure, for learning, for the beginnings of modern life. Fossil fuels power almost everything.
- **Type 0.8:** democracies give the vote to all citizens. Education and literacy spread worldwide and information becomes a valuable commodity. Energy demand is rampant, and some people have access to huge amounts and others to almost none. Some people still live at almost a 0.3 level, while others are pushing up to 0.9.
- **Type 0.9:** democracy begins to pervade more than just politics. Communications become democratic; inequalities become unsustainable. More stable, renewable and hugely powerful energy sources become available just as old, dirty ones become toxic and war-torn. Trade begins to make the world feel small and connected. The idea of globalisation emerges. Many people are safer but more stressed than ever before as the world changes rapidly. This is when crisis crossroads suddenly spring up. And the next step isn't inevitable; in fact, it's all too easy to slip back down the scale. But be smart and you can move up to…
- **Type 1:** made it! Globalism is based on worldwide wireless internet access, with all knowledge digitised and available to everyone. Institutions and mindsets shift into a new way of thinking about who we are. Individuals (not only companies or states) can trade globally, raising expectations of both personal freedom and collective interdependence. Billions are released from poverty to make the world a more diverse and fascinating place. Innovation and culture thrive. Fun matters. And it's all fuelled by abundant, clean, cheap energy that's available to everyone by tapping the Earth's own renewable power. Our planet becomes bright.

In 1973, the astronomer and writer Carl Sagan estimated that we were only a Type 0.7 global civilisation. More current assessments put us nearer 0.8, but only in some places. We can't reach Type 1 yet. It's impossible to get there with our current energy systems. There simply aren't enough oil, coal and gas to light up the planet for 7 billion people. Not even if we burned it all furiously. Access to energy pushes you up the scale, but without cheaper, cleaner energy in greater supplies, you hit a glass ceiling.

The forces dragging us back down the scale are the limits to current fossil-fuel energy and the big sucker punch of global warming. The things that will release us into Type 1 fun are all the changes we need to make to avoid climate change anyway.

For thousands of years, we have existed in a zero-sum world. One tribe, state or nation could only gain if another tribe, state or nation lost. Our politics, our institutions and even our identities all assume that's how things work. But change has been speeding up. It took millennia for humanity to get from 0.1 to 0.2, but then it only took 66 years between the first flight of a rickety plane by the Wright brothers to humanity sending a man to set foot on the moon. Now we need to get from 0.8 to Type 1 in one generation. And why wouldn't we want to? We deserve Type 1. So many people, from deniers to doom-mongers, theocracies and dictatorships, want to drag us back down the chain. They want to keep us in the dark.

I live in what's called a 'developed' country. Which is a terrible term because it suggests we have nothing else to strive for. That term assumes that what we have in places like Europe and the US represents the pinnacle of human progress and quality of life. That one little word sneaks into our head and suggests we've hit the peak and the only way is down. Or that those in 'developing' countries have only one option: to seek to live as we do. Both those mindsets place horrible constraints on our creativity. Instead, I believe that every country, every society and every person is developing. Reaching Type 1 would be the start of history. And there's so much more to come.

We Are Human

All this positive change is going to change something else: it's going to change us. Something very weird is going to happen: we're going to become human. Yes, I know technically we're all already human, but we're also a lot of other things. We're Russian, Vietnamese, American, Nigerian, English, Iranian, Samoan, etc. We're black, Asian, white, native and immigrant. We're women and men. We're the boss, the follower, the subordinate, the leader. We're admin assistants, CEOs, artists, cooks, homemakers, miners, farmers, shopkeepers, firemen, computer programmers, investment bankers and bricklayers.

We're so many different things. The fact that we're actually all human gets lost along the way. The superficial differences make it difficult to see our deep similarities. But Type 1 is a very human civilisation, one forged by fighting off the fire-breathing dragon of climate change that we created ourselves. We'll be a little singed, but we will know that we – all of us – are in this together. We'll have to cooperate as one species, and by doing so we'll learn about our collective power.

In the US, Italy, Argentina, South Africa, Russia and Iran[1] groups of researchers ran a very simple test on men and women aged between 18 and 75 years old, and from every background and income. The participants – in some countries wearing jeans, in others the hijab – all played a game. Each was given 10 tokens, which they could choose to place into either a personal, a national or a global 'account'. They then received a payout, depending on what everyone else had paid into. The game was set up so that the biggest payouts only happened when everyone cooperated and placed their tokens into the shared accounts. So if everyone paid into the global account, the payout was huge. But if most people kept their tokens only in their personal accounts, those who'd been global payers ended up losing much more than those who were selfish. No one knew what anyone else would do in advance. Getting a big reward was the incentive to cooperate, but that only happened if you thought globally and could trust that other participants would do the same.

Some played collaboratively, some selfishly. But the researchers weren't interested in those results; they were interested in the players themselves. And they found that across every culture, the people who paid into the global account turned out to have higher levels of trust, and contributed more than the researchers expected. But, more importantly, those 'global players' were always the happier and more satisfied human beings. That's the happy-hero mindset. These were

1. Nancy R. Buchan et al., 'Globalization and Human Cooperation', *Proceedings of the National Academy of Sciences of the United States of America*, 106.11 (2009): 4138–42.

the people who knew they were human first. They knew that the only way to win is together.

League of Heroes

Getting to Type 1 is going to take billions of heroes working through their squabbles and disagreements together and getting over their prejudices, because cooperation is simply the only way. And by doing that we'll change how we see each other. We'll beat climate change, and at the same time, we will forge a sense of human identity. We'll realise how amazing we really are and how amazing everyone else is. Changing the world will forge us into a team. I know for a fact how awesome that team is, and I want you to come and join it.

That's what I'm asking of you as we come to the end of our hero's journey: to change yourself for good and feel better for a lifetime. Sometimes you might forget, get distracted or let denial or doom beat you back. That happens to everyone. But now you know how amazing it feels to make a difference. And that feeling is always waiting for you.

Then What?

You know what we're up against, and you know we are going to make it. You all know how important you are, and you're ready to help each other. You're going to keep your eyes fixed steadfastly on our amazing future as you climb the crisis curve. You're going to be happy and you're going to act heroically. And I'm going to be right there beside you.

We're going be the generation who sees over the horizon. We're going to change the world for the better and become a Type 1 civilisation. And that's going to be marvellous. Billions of well fed, healthy, educated humans, all experiencing a species-level shot of self-esteem and looking around at the view, wondering what to do next.

Will we…

... Talk to Each Other?

Perhaps we'll travel around the world and explore it. Create an explosion of communications and discover the wild and wonderful. Go to all those exotic places we've always wanted to see. Meet all the people and cultures we've wondered about. Ask questions. Learn. See everything and meet everyone. Work out what this 'being human' thing really means.

... Find Someone New to Talk to?

This is my favourite. Let's go out into the universe and find our neighbours! Work out if we're really alone here in space, or if we are just too young to be taken seriously. Perhaps we'll find some Type 2s and 3s out there, somewhere.

... Make Someone to Talk to?

Perhaps we'll throw our ingenuity, our energy and our creativity into one great endeavour. Every year we're getting closer to creating true artificial intelligence. We could make a new type of mind to talk to. I wonder what we'll say to each other?

... Reflect on It All?

Or we'll need a breather. A moment to reflect and rest after the effort of conquering the crisis curve. To be spiritual. To be quiet. To be.

... Party?

But if I had to lay a bet, then I think that when we get to Type 1, we'll do one thing more than any other: I think we'll have fun. We'll create mind-blowing games, new experiences, big ideas and global competitions. The Olympics, the World Cup, the Super Bowl and a big Saturday night out will be nothing compared to this. We'll have something to celebrate. And the party might last a generation.

Actually, we probably won't do any of these things. Or we'll do all of them, but in a totally unexpected way. The only thing you can be sure of is that we'll do something amazing. Because we are amazing.

Because you are amazing.

Now go save the damn planet.

*

The Story of a Happy Hero

'Wait!' Jane found herself on her feet in the middle of the town hall. 'Excuse me, but I'm not from London. I was born and raised here. And I think we should build that wind farm.' She swallowed nervously and went on, trying to speak loudly enough for everyone in the large hall to hear. 'I don't fully understand some of what's been said, but I do know that renewable energy is safer, cleaner and getting cheaper. It's important.' Jane looked down at Ben, who was wide-eyed at seeing his mum arguing with the MP. 'My son and I have been really looking into this. And for his sake, and for our whole town, I believe we should be at the forefront of change, showing other towns how it's done.'

The MP looked darkly at her for a moment and then his smile spread again. 'Well, ma'am, not that I want to cast aspersions on your own or your little boy's expertise, but I think the arguments we've heard today show that delaying is simply the best option, for everybody.' His smile seemed to take in the whole room.

As Jane stood there she could feel her body practically vibrate with a mixture of indignation and embarrassment. The MP just looked relaxed, smiling, waiting for her to sit down. As Jane tried to settle her thoughts and come back with another argument, she heard a distinct 'harrumph' beside her. Her dad had got to his feet, pausing for a moment before slowly starting to speak.

'No. The way I see it… there's been enough things delayed around here already by you and your like. Now I'm no fan of all this climate-change talk and what have you, but I'm all for local jobs and keeping ahead of things, for the young folks' sake. I'm a local man, and I say… get on with it.'

'Hear, hear!' Jane spun around to see her CEO standing at the back of the room, along with several other smartly dressed executives. 'I'm here to represent our local chamber of commerce,' the CEO went on. 'All these business leaders and I have joined this meeting with the express intention of encouraging the development of the proposed wind farm. Or as that gentleman said so well, we want you to just get on with it!'

Several people in the room now started to stand, including Aunty Em, Chris and Ben. One person called out: 'It's already got planning permission, what's the delay for anyway?' And Aunty Em said loudly: 'Ben wants his wind farm!' which raised a few questioning eyebrows on people nearby, but brought a big grin from Ben himself.

'Right,' said Jane over the din, quietening everyone down. 'It seems us locals don't want a delay. And unless you want to test whether we want *you*, I suggest you back us up.'

The MP looked distinctly uncomfortable and shot a look at one of the grey-suited men. But then his political training caught up with him and he said smoothly: 'Of course, of course, there is clearly strong feeling in the room. Perhaps a delay isn't necessary. I'll raise your thoughts with the planning committee.'

'You'd better,' Aunty Em said. 'I'm a little old lady with time on my hands, and I'm going to come to all those public meetings and watch your every move like a hawk. And if I don't like what I see, then I'm reporting back to her!' She stabbed her thumb towards Jane, which made Ben burst out laughing.

Outside the town hall it took a while to get back to the car. So many people wanted to give Jane's family their contact details and congratulations. When they finally reached it, Dad climbed in as if nothing had happened, and Chris gave her a big wink as he got Ben in. Jane gave her Aunty Em a massive hug.

'Now then,' Aunty Em said softly. 'No need for that now. I always knew you had it in you.'

'I can't believe I did it!' Jane said.

'Well,' Aunty Em replied, 'I can, and I know your mum would be proud too. I might not be a parent myself, but I know what she would think. In fact' – she looked a little sly – 'I know what the Godmother would think.'

Aunty Em gave her a mischievous grin, and Jane burst out laughing.

Acknowledgements

This book only exists because of the generosity and positivity of others. Most especially the supporters who crowdfunded the book over just one weekend! Heartfelt thanks to you all. And to Paul Edmondson and Sarah Hosking at the Hosking Houses Trust for the invaluable space to write. To David Martin for research and insight. To 16 years of Futerrans for honing these ideas with me, and to Ed Gillespie, Lucy Shea, Freya Williams and Karen Brennen for making Futerra what it is. Thanks, hugs and much more owed to Kaj Torok, Jonathon Porritt, Charlie at Urban Writers, Liza Ravenscroft, Warren Beeby, Stefan Kyriazis, Jo Confino, Lucy Siegle, Tony Juniper, Chris Pennington and Sarah Holloway. Deep gratitude to my editor Anne, Xander and all at Unbound for your belief and bravery. And, of course, everlasting thanks and love to my parents Deborah and Patrick Townsend for teaching me heroism, and my sisters Sian and Francesca for every day.

Patrons List

Carla Alzamora
Charlotte Bladh André
Kate Andrews
Warren Beeby
David Bent
Linda Blom
Gian Maria Bruno
Lucy Carver
Elaine Chambers
Tracey Rawling Church
Ali Clabburn (Liftshare)
Melanie Coath
Maggie Cooper
Sarah Corbett
Ben Costley
Laurence Cox
Alanna Curtin
Michael Davies
Bex Dawkes
Christian De Boisredon
Paul Edmondson
Emma Fieldhouse
Liv Fjellander
Briony Gittins
John Grant
Sarah Holloway
Caroline Hudson
Jennifer Johnson
Raechel Kelly
Geoff Kendall
Christina Kennedy
Oliver Ingwall King

Casper ter Kuile
Lucy Langdon
Janice Lao
Oliver Lawder
Joel Makower
Kaj Meerstadt
Amy Mount
Sally Osborn
Cara Parish
Sara Parkin
Jonathan Perugia
Francesca Phillips
Terry-paul Phillips
Cyndi Rhoades
Christoph Sander
Blandine Surry-Stefani
Hermione Taylor
Manon Thomas
Jerker Thorsell
Lynette Thorstensen
Matthew Van Den Elst
Joanna Walton
Sue Webster
David Willans
Louise Wilson
Martin Wright
Joanna Yarrow
Hollie Zecca

Action Advocate Page

ACTION ADVOCATE:
FOOD FOR PROGRESS

A Progress Poem

We are progress addicts
On the journey of life
We've found our drug
Which makes us high
And it's all about people
Who kick progress alive

We are progress addicts
With just one fear
That we'll keep on tearing
This globe straight to hell
Even though we can tell
That the way to react
Is to make progress act

So we keep on doing
Keep on talking
So we raise our kids to act
Be people who react
We want them to feel high
on kicking progress alive.

How can you feel this every day? Food is on every human beings agenda every day. Therefore it as a powerful tool to get people into that addictive feeling of doing good. How? Serve your self a really tasty sustainable meal. And above all share that tasty food with the people we love! Just with our grandma, or all our coolest friends at a party. Then talk about that awesome sustainable food. Make them notice that addictive feeling of doing good. The cravings for doing good have a potential to spread to all areas of life. Just like any other addiction. And yes, Sharing with friends is a truly joyful way of changing the world. To spread the progress addiction!

Food for Progress is driving a new food logic. The goal? Healthy, tasty and nutritious food that everyone on the planet can eat, forever. We need to eat in a way that allows us all to thrive within the planetary boundaries. Action is now!

www.foodforprogress.com

Food for Progress pledged on Unbound.com as the Action Advocate for this book.